FIRST STEPS
into
HEALING

NORMAL EVERYDAY CHRISTIAN LIFE

Dennis Acott

 Zaccmedia

Published by Zaccmedia
www.zaccmedia.com
info@zaccmedia.com

Published August 2018

ISBN: 978-1-911211-84-6

British Library Cataloguing-in-Publication Data
A catalogue record for this book is available from the British Library.

CONTENTS

INTRODUCTION

And these signs will accompany those who believe ... they will place
their hands on sick people, and they will get well.

(Mark 16:17, 18, NIV 1984)

THEY SAY THAT THE BEST PLACE to start is at the beginning, but life is full of new beginnings, isn't it? This book is going to start at a very special new beginning for us – my wife Cathy and me. This was the time when the seeds were first sown for Eagles 4031, the Christian ministry we founded together, after experiencing an amazing, miraculous healing encounter with the power of God.

Soon after this wonderful event took place, Holy Spirit[1] clearly directed us to Matthew 10:7–8. The last sentence of this passage had a special impact upon our spirits and we somehow just knew that God was stirring up something new within us.

> As you go, proclaim this message: 'The kingdom of heaven has come near.' Heal those who are ill, raise the dead, cleanse those who have leprosy, drive out demons. **Freely you have received; freely give.**[2]

Yes, we had freely received a healing miracle and, glorious though this was, it seemed clear that it was never intended to be an end in itself. Over time we began to understand that God gives to us in order that we may give away to others what we have received from Him. And because He is eternal, and His resources are infinite, no matter how much we may give away there will never be any lack of supply on His part. There is always more for us to draw upon from His deep, deep wells.

You probably know that the instruction 'Be filled with the Spirit' (Ephesians 5:18) means, in effect, 'Be *being* filled'. So, it is not intended to be a once and forever experience but an ongoing, oft-repeated experience because, as already stated, there is always more in Heaven's economy. As we continue to be being filled with the Spirit, so we will continue to be being equipped to give away what Holy Spirit wants to minister, both to us and through us.

We came to realise that what began as a single, incredible healing encounter, which blessed both of us, could develop into multiple healing experiences to bless others. We have all been entrusted with a never-ending Kingdom 'chequebook' that we can use, as directed, to draw on the infinite resources of the Lord to bless those He leads us to.

It is certainly not false humility to suggest that Cathy and I are no more special in the Kingdom of Heaven than any other Christian. This simple realisation helped lead us into the understanding that what God was calling and enabling us to do is equally possible for every other born-again, spirit-filled Christian living on this planet. That seems so simple, so obvious, yet it is evidently not something that every Christian is taught, takes on board, or lives out.

We became very aware that not only should we be giving away freely what we had been freely given but also that we were to encourage other Christians to do the same. We began by taking every opportunity given to us to share our healing testimony, hoping to help motivate all those who heard us to step out in faith in just the same way God was calling and equipping us to do. What we found was that most people would rejoice with us over our testimony but, for whatever reason, few of them seemed to 'get' what, to us, was the most important part. Most seemed disinclined to step out in faith themselves.

Had we misunderstood what we believed God was calling us to do? Had we simply been presumptuous? Had we been carried away by our own euphoria? Who did we think we were?

All sorts of negative thoughts and questions like this assailed us but, thanks to the timely, prophetic encouragements of several of our Christian friends, we quickly learned to press on. After all, some degree of spiritual opposition is an inevitable consequence of deciding to trust God and step out in faith in any way. It was important to remain positive, to press on and to seek Him for the path forward.

God led us into some new ministry opportunities locally and into new connections within the wider Christian family, each one being designed to educate us and to broaden our knowledge and **experience**. We came across new books and other media that spoke the same language and encouraged us greatly.

Researching two thousand years of healing ministry within church history was an inspiration. Coming to terms with **disappointments** proved to be an essential part of the early learning curve too as, my research confirms, only Jesus has a 100% success record in healing.

Another Bible verse which has proved to be an essential part
of our armoury is John 14:12, quoting the words of Jesus:

> I tell you the truth, **anyone** who has faith in me will do
> what I have been doing. He [or she] will do even **greater**
> things than these, because I am going to the Father.

(NIV 1984)

If this sounds unrealistic, remember that we don't need faith to
do what is possible. It is outside of our comfort zones that great
things happen!

It is so important for us to understand that Jesus Himself (who
said 'I am ... the truth', John 14:6) has promised that we can and
will do the things He did, if we have faith in Him – and put that
faith into action. Who wants to look in a mirror, then walk away,
forgetting what they look like? (See James 1:23–24.)

He declares that we can do even greater things, too! Now, we
can either spend time speculating on what those 'greater things'
might be, or we can find out by simply getting out there and doing
'the stuff' (as John Wimber memorably expressed it)! We need to
come to a realisation that what we are seeking to do *is* in the will
of God, knowing we are free to do it, and that He *will* back us up
(Mark 16:20).

So, please read on and let me share our (my and Cathy's)
experiences with you. We want to encourage you to 'step out of the
boat'. We do not claim to be doing this as experts but as ordinary
people doing our best to follow the call of God, learning as we go.
We believe that this call is on your life just as surely as it is on ours.
We know very well that we are no more 'important' than you are.

If you are not doing so already, will you at least consider joining
us in rising to the challenge set before every believer? After all,

this is how 'Acts 29' gets to be written, and this new chapter really does include your story as well as ours.

NOTES

[1] Whenever Holy Spirit is referred to in the text of this book, apart from in some quotations from the Bible or other sources, I have chosen not to include the word 'the' beforehand. Some may find this strange, even pernickety. Others will agree that to put 'the' before the Name of the third Person of the Trinity just does not seem to be honouring Him.

[2] All emphasis within scripture quotations is my own.

Chapter 1

———————————■———————————

HEALING
TESTIMONY

*Those who hope in the LORD will renew their strength. They will
soar on wings like eagles; they will run and not grow weary, they
will walk and not be faint.*

(Isaiah 40:31)

ONCE YOU HAVE READ THE FOLLOWING, and
linked it with the verse quoted above, you will not find
it at all difficult to work out where the inspiration for our
Eagles 4031 ministry name came from. You will also understand
why these magnificent creatures have such significance in our lives
since that special evening in May 2008 when we sat down to watch
GOD TV. Already we have two original paintings of eagles, by
talented Christian artists, hanging on the walls at home!

But let's go back to that new beginning to put everything into
context. Cathy and I married on 28 December 1996, a second
(and last!) marriage for both of us. Not long afterwards – we are

1

not sure if it was in early 1997 or 1998 – I suffered some sort of viral illness. As you would expect, it laid me low for a few days. The trouble was, I never seemed able to shake off the effects completely. Life continued pretty much as normal, but I always had this problem with never feeling 100% healthy. I was constantly tired and lethargic, not exactly full of beans. It was a puzzle, a real cause for concern.

We had both been Christians for many years and we knew that Jesus healed people, as in the Gospel accounts, and that, even today, some people still got healed – although they usually seemed to live in so-called 'developing' countries!

I had gained a few years' experience of healing through serving on ministry teams, even before I met Cathy, but this was invariably of the inner healing variety (emotional issues and the like). Examples of physical healing were extremely rare, at least in my personal experience. The cultural norm, in the circles I had moved in, was to rely exclusively upon the medical profession for help. So that is what we did, too, to try to find a solution to my puzzle.

Over a period of several years, I was subjected to all manner of medical tests and experiments, some of them during hospital appointments. The only meaningful thing that was discovered, after a minor operation to obtain, for analysis, a sample of liver tissue, was a slight fault in my liver function. That was quite easily and quickly rectified by a simple modification to my diet.

There must have been some adverse effect on my immune system also, because I became much more susceptible to whatever 'bug' or ailment was currently doing the rounds. It was also more difficult for me to cope with pressure, particularly at work. So much so that, in late 2004, I suffered 'burn-out', possibly a minor nervous breakdown, which resulted in me having to take a total of five weeks off work.

There was one occasion when Cathy was going to make a drink and she asked me if I wanted one. When I answered in the affirmative she enquired if I would prefer tea or coffee. That simple choice proved to be too much for me to cope with and I simply broke down in tears! This was particularly worrying as I had always been rather 'British' as far as displaying emotions was concerned. My upper lip tended towards stiffening rather than quivering!

About 12 months after this, I started having coughing sessions. This did not seem to be an undue cause for concern until, one day, while going upstairs to the bathroom, I coughed and blacked out, falling backwards down the stairs, headfirst into a radiator at the bottom. Cathy, in the middle of making Christmas cake and pudding in the kitchen, rushed into the hallway where she found me unconscious on the floor.

She tried to engage me in conversation, to check me out, but I made even less sense than usual! Eventually I remembered the reason for my aborted trip upstairs. Cathy suggested it might be wiser for me to visit the downstairs toilet instead. Apparently, I stayed in there for so long she had to come and rescue me. My purpose for going in there had been completely forgotten!

After ringing our GP, Cathy took his advice to get me to the local hospital for a check-up. I just about recovered sufficiently in time to direct her to the rear car park as she had found the main one to be full. Cathy is not a happy driver and admits she is not blessed with much of a sense of direction. There was no real damage done to me, so it turned out, just mild concussion.

A subsequent visit to our own doctor led to a diagnosis of 'cough syncope',[1] and I was only the third case of this unusual malady he had encountered. The second one involved a person sitting outside in the waiting room at that very moment! The doctor kindly taught me what to do when I sensed that a coughing bout was imminent so that it would not result in me fainting.

I could not be left at home alone, just in case, so Cathy was signed off from work to be with me 24/7. We both lost a lot of sleep until the symptoms finally wore off. I returned to work, probably too early, half asleep and unable to speak other than in a very hoarse whisper. Mind you, I got through a lot of ice cream to soothe my exceptionally sore throat!

Once every other possibility had been discounted, the medical profession finally decided that I had ME (also known as chronic fatigue syndrome).[2] I was informed that there is no cure for this condition but there were various aids available to enable me to learn how to manage it. Later research has revealed that something like 6% of people can make a full recovery, but there is a high likelihood of regression and the best hope is that the condition will plateau out at a manageable level. Some people are so badly affected that they do not even have the strength to lift a cup of tea to their lips!

Although I did experience deterioration from this point onwards, my condition was never such that I had to give up work. However, I did have to shed some responsibilities and be very careful about keeping to 'normal' office hours. Even so, this gradually led to a state of exhaustion most evenings and weekends. Obviously, this impacted on our social life, not to mention having to cut back on church commitments like preaching, ministry team and home-group leading.

I was probably at my lowest ebb as we moved into 2008. Cathy was by now taking on the whole burden of running our home as well as continuing in her very demanding job as a primary school teacher. Unknown to me, she was pretty much at her wits' end by the time we managed to fit in a holiday at Easter 2008. I was able to enjoy some of our time away in one of our favourite UK seaside resorts (Southwold, in Suffolk) but the second week proved to be rather more of a struggle than a joy.

Soon after we returned home, we picked up an answer-phone message, from our friends Laurence and Chris, asking if we had been watching the 'Lakeland, Florida Outpouring' on GOD TV. They went on to recommend that, if we had missed it so far, we should put that right as soon as possible. They informed us that large numbers of people were being healed, including those who were just watching from home! By this time, the event was being screened on GOD TV every evening, so we did not have to wait very long to tune in for the first time.

I must be honest and say that it took a few viewings to adjust to the style of presentation, and the appearance of the speaker, to conclude that it was 'kosher' (in our opinion). We noticed that Todd Bentley normally ministered by means of words of knowledge (1 Corinthians 12:8) and that people in the auditorium were usually healed in their seats before coming to the platform to testify. Only then were they prayed for, most of them falling in the Spirit, something we had both witnessed before, but not regularly. Later, we became aware that this was how Kathryn Kuhlman operated. During the programmes, written testimonies from viewers were shown moving across the bottom of the screen, all verifying the truth of what we had been told.

Almost every evening, as we began to watch the broadcasts, Todd at some point called out 'chronic fatigue', as a word of knowledge, but this did not resonate with me on any of those occasions. On what was probably about the fourth night that we tuned in, however, he coupled 'chronic fatigue' with 'spirit of infirmity' and that really did register in my spirit. I told Cathy that I was certain these combined words of knowledge were intended for me. As we wondered how to respond, Todd said something like, 'If anyone watching at home is reacting to any of these words, then get up out of your seat, touch your television screen, and God will heal you.'

Cathy looked at me expectantly, but I was thinking, *Oh, come on! That's silly! I'm not doing that!* As those words ran through my mind I believe the Lord reminded me of the story of Naaman the Syrian (2 Kings 5) and that changed my attitude immediately. I thought, *If I'm going to look like an idiot, only Cathy and I are here, and she isn't going to be shocked by that revelation!*

So, I grabbed her hand, got up from the settee, walked around the coffee table, skirted round the edge of an armchair, touched the TV screen and ... nothing happened!

Almost at once, I just 'knew'[3] (God at work again, in my spirit, I believe) that Cathy had to touch the screen as well, so I asked her to do so. The moment she did: *BANG!* It was like 10,000 volts of electricity hit me!

I flew headfirst backwards across the room, past the armchair, over the coffee table and on to the settee that I had just vacated! I bounced up and down and shook from head to foot! Meanwhile, unknown to me, Cathy was flat out on the floor on the other side of the room! This was the first time she had gone down in the Spirit!

Back on the settee, I felt like something came up and out from my chest. Somehow, I knew (godly revelation again?) that it was the awful spirit of infirmity leaving me! *Wow!* This was really going to take some processing, but there was no denying that the power of God was at work in our lounge that night!

In the days that followed there were various proofs that my ordeal was over. One such was the following Sunday morning. I was scheduled to preach at a small local fellowship, not my home church. For some time now any such activity would be a joy to do, but it would always leave me totally exhausted afterwards, unable to manage anything else for the rest of the day.

As part of what I had to say, I shared my testimony of what had happened to me. Cathy and I found ourselves being asked to pray, after the meeting, for anyone who needed healing. We were led into a separate room, where the children had been having their own activities earlier. Whoever wanted prayer was to wait outside and then come in one at a time to be ministered to.

We thought we might have two or three people queuing to see us, but we ended up praying with most of the congregation – or so it seemed. What a privilege! Then we went home for a very late lunch, following which I attacked a pile of ironing – and still was not tired! Praise the Lord – He does all things perfectly!

Somehow, we knew that there must be more to this than a wonderful healing, but we had no idea what it could be or how it would come about. We just wanted to serve the Lord and do anything He wanted us to do. It would have to be a case of waiting patiently (never easy for me!) for Him to reveal His purposes for us. This He began to do in stages and, over the next year or so, what was to become Eagles 4031 gradually took shape.

Since that marvellous, unforgettable evening in May 2008, we have both learned and experienced so much and our heart's desire is to share what we can from this to encourage every single Christian we meet.

Maybe you have never stepped out to minister to the sick before. Maybe you have, but you have been disappointed by an apparent lack of positive results. Maybe you are part of a church family that does not believe this ministry is for today. Or maybe you just need a little bit of encouragement to press on in faithful persistence.

Whatever your reason for reading this book, my prayer is that you will stay with it to the end, be blessed and become a blessing, motivated by love and compassion to bring healing to others.

NOTES

[1] Cough syncope results in loss of consciousness during episodes of coughing.

[2] ME is the neurological disease myalgic encephalomyelitis, also known as chronic fatigue syndrome.

[3] The sense of 'knowing' here is, in my view, either a 'word of knowledge' (see Chapter 3) or another form of revelation from Holy Spirit.

Chapter 2

GOING OUT
ON A LIMB

*Taking him by the right hand, [Peter] helped him up, and instantly
the man's feet and ankles became strong.*

(Acts 3:7)

'I THINK YOU MIGHT FIND THIS INTERESTING,' *Elise*[1] said to me one Sunday, at the end of the morning service, handing me a package that contained a very ancient-looking videotape. Cathy and I studied it when we got home. It was clearly a copy, not an original, and the only label on it was a sticky one on the spine with the words 'Growing Out Arms and Legs' written on it. We put it to one side, intending to view it sometime, maybe, possibly, perhaps.

The next evening, I was at a Parochial Church Council meeting. Towards the end of it, the vicar announced that the following weekend a ministry called 'Healing on the Streets' (HoTS)[2] would be offering training. This would be held on Friday evening and also during the day on Saturday. Anyone interested was invited to pick up a leaflet and take it from there. I picked up a leaflet and we (both) took it from there.

This happened in the summer of 2009, just over a year after the ME power encounter, when we knew that the Lord was calling us into something to do with healing but, so far, we were not sure what form it would take. In the meantime, any opportunity to learn more about the healing ministry was grabbed with our four hands. Cathy and I booked in for the training that would take place in a church at Tankerton, near Whitstable on the north Kent coast, about 40 minutes' drive from our home in Maidstone.

Our progress, at this point, was pretty much limited to setting up a house group in our home. This was with the primary aim of exploring the healing ministry in the Bible and what it means for us today. A few like-minded friends had joined us and, to be fair, we had probably not progressed very much. We were 'limited' to worshipping and studying but saw some of the gifts of Holy Spirit manifested as we ministered to one another.

Before going to the first training meeting, Cathy and I did find time to have a quick look at the beginning of that video. It featured an American couple called Charles and Frances Hunter, what appeared to be a teaching ministry involving healing, and referred to events called 'Healing Explosions'. The bit we had time to view showed someone who seemed to have arms of differing lengths and, when prayed for, they evened up, to the same length, as we watched. We were amazed, but wary – having never heard of this couple before and the filming obviously having taken place some years previously, judging by the style of clothing worn by the various participants.

It was an interesting and enjoyable Friday evening at the healing course and we looked forward to learning more the next day. Part way through Saturday morning Mark Marx, the person doing most of the teaching (and who turned out to be the founder of the Healing on the Streets ministry), asked if there was anyone present suffering from back pain. A man put his hand up and was invited to the front, where he was asked to sit down in a chair facing the rest of us.

Mark called for the camera, which was recording proceedings, to be brought near so that it was focused on the man's legs and feet. That seemed most strange to me (if he had a back problem) but, hey, we were there to learn. Then he 'measured' the man's legs by holding them in his hands!

Mark asked the cameraman to focus on both feet from one side of the room. This was so that everyone could see what was happening on the screen if they could not get close enough to the action. The man was wearing white trainers with very thick soles and it became obvious that one leg was shorter than the other by about the depth of one of the soles. Mark then commanded the short leg to grow out to match the length of the other one, in the name of Jesus. *And it did!*

We guessed this must be what that video was about. It must work with both arms and legs. We decided that we would be watching the whole of that video when we got home. The training ended at lunchtime but, after lunch, we were to go into nearby Whitstable. There we would set up a Healing on the Streets site on the forecourt of the Anglican church in the high street.

I'll come back to that, but let me mention now that, during a rare quiet spell in the afternoon, I went up to the man whose back had been ministered to (via his legs) to ask a few questions to check things out for myself. To cut a long story short, I was satisfied that he used to have a serious back problem. The adjustment to his legs (which had corrected skeletal misalignment) had resulted in the eradication of pain and his complete healing. Hallelujah!

When we got to the church we found that it had a sort of garden at the front and a wide, paved area that went from the church doors to the pavement of the high street, some 10–15 metres. Mark had a banner erected near the pavement with 'Healing' printed on it in large, bold letters. No pressure there then! He had us set up a dozen chairs along the path, six on each side. Volunteers were recruited to hand out leaflets on the street and to direct people onto the church forecourt if they agreed to be prayed for.

Interestingly, before we did anything else, he got us all to kneel on the ground, telling us that we would not be getting up again until we all felt the presence of Holy Spirit. *That's pushing it a bit*, I thought. But I was wrong. We all experienced the tangible presence of the Lord within less than two minutes of kneeling down. Later in the afternoon Cathy had to go back to our car for something or other and she said she could really feel a major change in the atmosphere between the church forecourt area and elsewhere!

We learned that the presence of God is essential for healing grace to be manifested, as God is more than just the Healer – He *is* Healing. This was our first lesson in making it a priority to cultivate His presence before actively moving into a time of healing ministry. You must understand that all this was very new to us then. We were treading on new ground at the beginning of a major learning curve – but we were up for it! This was so exciting – and we hadn't even ministered to anyone there yet!

Then various people began to come off the street for prayer. They sat in the chairs and, because it was a large team, three or four of us gathered around each one to minister to them. During the afternoon, we probably ministered for no more than two hours and there were several testimonies from people who had either been healed or blessed by God in some other way.

Incidentally, Mark said that the arrangement with the local churches, whose folk had participated in the training, was that this was to be the first of a regular, weekly time for Healing on the Streets ministry to take place, same time, same location, every Saturday. He emphasised that local people needed to know this was not just a one-off, that they could trust the Christians to be there for them on a regular basis. So, this was the plan going forward.

When Cathy and I got home we did watch the video and we did some research to find out who this Charles and Frances Hunter were.[3] Just briefly, let me say here that they were possibly the first healing evangelists to involve ordinary believers in their ministry as a matter of normal practice rather than having everyone come only to them on the platform for healing. They would spend a few days in a city training those who wanted to learn how to minister healing effectively and then, at the weekend, they would hold a 'Healing Explosion' meeting in a large public venue. When the time for ministering healing came, they would invite people to come forward to be ministered to – by the team who had been trained during the week.

Shortly after our weekend in Tankerton and Whitstable we discovered that Frances Hunter had just died, at the age of 93 years. Charles died about 12 months later, aged 90 years. The video was probably from the early 1980s and, over time, we managed to get additional video and printed material to learn more about their amazing ministry and how God used them so mightily to mobilise members of the Body of Christ to get their hands dirty rather than to just sit in the pews, or chairs, as passive spectators. We drew real inspiration from all this. Incidentally, their daughter, Joan Hunter, still has an active, itinerant healing ministry.

We shared this experience with our home group and experimented together, slightly limited by the fact that we all seemed to have arms and legs of even lengths! Nevertheless, we sensed the presence of God with us and this was encouraging as we moved into the summer break.

The following month we were back on ministry team duty at the (then) annual Detling Summer Celebration, held at the Kent County Showground. This event was spread over six days, Saturday to Thursday, and the attendance was numbered in hundreds. There were morning and evening celebrations with guest speakers, powerful worship, an array of workshops and a variety of 'after hours' entertainment; all in all, a very packed programme.

The first ministry session we were involved in found Cathy and me praying for a man who limped in and asked for a chair to sit on, as he was not able to remain standing for long because it was too painful for him. Normal practice was to minister standing up, as it was felt that sitting with people could encourage team members to move into 'counselling mode' and this was neither the time nor the place for that. Not to mention that few, if any, of us would be suitably qualified! The next day, and every day after that for the rest of the week, this gentleman was seen jogging around the showground − praise the Lord! But some exciting things, more in keeping with the subject of this chapter, were still to come.

The ministry team was expected to be on hand at the end of the main morning and evening meetings, in case there were people asking for prayer for any reason, and also at the end of some of the seminars that were more likely than others to provoke such a response. At the close of a meeting, just before lunch one day, we got into conversation with a woman and her husband who had been members of our home church before *Roger* went off to 'vicar school'. The couple who had called us about the GOD TV broadcasts, Laurence and Chris, were also present.

During the conversation, we learned that *Sandra* had been in a car accident and suffered a whiplash injury that was still giving her problems, so we offered to pray for her. Holy Spirit 'zapped' her very quickly and she was lying on the floor for about half an

hour while He ministered to every part of her skeletal structure
from head to toe.

When she got back to her feet she felt so much better and asked
if we could pray for a friend who was on site and had suffered
in the same way. We suggested that the friend should meet us in
a seminar that afternoon, which was to be conducted by Arnold
Muwonge[4] and Paul Bennison.[5] We knew that the meeting would
almost certainly be given over to prayer and healing ministry at
some point. Other ministry team members would also be present
to support Arnold and Paul.

We met this lady, ministered to her, and God did for her
what he had done for Sandra. There was opportunity to minister
to several other people with skeletal problems, one or two of
whom had arms of uneven length when we started. We had still
to encounter any wonky legs and, indeed, that was not to happen
for a few more months.

One special healing that remains firmly in my mind, though,
involved the same young lady mentioned elsewhere who helped me
with the girl in pixie boots (see Chapter 3). I don't remember how
it came about now but we found ourselves ministering to a pelvic
problem – the first of many we have encountered over the years
since, and which proved to be our introduction to the phenomenon
we have called 'hula-hooping'!

We have learned that one of the ways of identifying someone
who may have a misaligned pelvis is by observing the way they
stand or walk. Someone who is pigeon-toed may well have a
pelvis that is turned in too much and the opposite could be true of
someone who has the classic Charlie Chaplin walk. When healing is
ministered to such people they invariably find that their body begins
to undulate like a Hawaiian dancer or a person hula-hooping!

We try to explain that this is the equivalent of half a dozen
expensive sessions with a chiropractor condensed into a few minutes,

and for free, by Holy Spirit. This is exactly what happened to *Karen*, in quite dramatic style, but she laughingly accused Cathy of being responsible for her movements. When Cathy removed her hands, which had been laid on Karen's hips, and the movements continued unabated, she conceded that God must be at work!

At the end of the morning session mentioned earlier, just before we went to lunch, Laurence and Chris asked if they could pray for us while we were still in the main arena. Of course, we agreed immediately, not knowing that they were going to pray that the Lord would allow the Hunters' 'mantle' (2 Kings 2) to fall upon us! The power of God hit us both and I remember skidding headfirst along the tarpaulin ground-covering and under the front row of chairs! From this experience, the video and the other things that happened, we deduced that God was calling us to do something like the Hunters had done, and that the healing of misaligned skeletons and shortened limbs would form a major part of the ministry we ourselves would exercise.

This has proved to be the case and we have had such exciting and rewarding times ever since, just watching God at work. Our conviction, like that of the Hunters, that the healing ministry is for *all* believers, rather than just some chosen few, continues undiminished – despite the many frustrations that we have encountered. Let's face it; if you are obedient to the call of God there is someone (the devil) who is not exactly pleased about it! We have learned the hard way that opposition is inevitable, but that encouragement can be derived even from this – praise the Lord!

I feel prompted to include a story from a weekend of Eagles 4031 ministry, at a church not 30 minutes' drive from our home in Kent. We had been made aware beforehand that *Chas*, the worship leader, had various health issues and his friends wondered if he would come forward for ministry. He did, possibly after a little persuasion by one of those friends. This happened while members of the congregation were ministering healing to one another after they had been given and shared words of knowledge, some of them for the first time. The front of the church was getting busy, so I was asked to help by joining Chas and the person who brought him forward.

I felt led to 'brush off' from him the disappointment of not seeming to have received any signs of improved health despite being prayed for many times over a period of years. Chas immediately groaned and sank to the floor. It seemed right to leave him there in the presence of the Lord to do some 'personal business' with Him. He remained stretched out on the carpet for about 20 minutes, by which time almost everyone else had left the building.

I went over to check that Chas was OK and I can't remember now which one of us said something that prompted me to ask if I could check out the possibility that his body was out of alignment. It may have been when he spoke about lower back pain, but there was such a catalogue of health issues that I cannot be sure now. Suffice it to say that, upon checking him out (unscientifically), one leg was clearly shorter than the other, probably by almost an inch.

As I ministered to him we both saw the 'short' leg 'grow out'. He then made mention of upper back and neck pain, so I asked if I could check out his arms. This proved to have been Holy Spirit inspired, as one arm clearly appeared to be about two inches 'shorter' than the other. That very soon 'grew out' also and, when he stood up and flexed his body, he was immediately aware of the difference the Lord had made and he also felt better in himself.

I do not remember ever having come across anyone else, to date, who has had skeletal misalignment indicated through both arms and legs at the same time. Incidentally, he was the first person with misaligned arms I had encountered for quite some time. It seemed to be almost always arms in the beginning but, for some while, only legs. Please forgive me as I fail to resist the temptation to declare that God's grace is *limb*-itless!

The next day Chas kindly volunteered to provide a testimony in the Sunday morning healing service and, quite rightly, he finished by saying that he was still a work in progress. The exciting change was that he was now full of expectant faith that God would bring to completion the good work He had begun in him by dealing with his various other ailments.

Over the years, we have seen God heal many people by skeletal realignment and, for want of a better term, this has become a sort of 'speciality'. Other ministry team members, who know us well, tended to refer such cases to us because of our history, with God, in this context. Do not be surprised if you find that there is a certain ailment or condition that becomes a sort of 'speciality' of yours over time. Far from encouraging independence, this should serve as a greater incentive to work as teams serving the Lord.

God has gained a reputation for moving in 'mysterious ways' and we recently encountered a classic example of this. During an Eagles 4031 ministry weekend, while I was teaching, I referred in passing to both scoliosis and a misaligned leg. Using a speaker's 'trick' to personalise my remarks, I gave the impression of addressing these examples directly to a specific person, someone whom I had not met before and knew nothing about.

During a break at the end of that session, another person in the group approached me. She wanted to know if I was aware that the lady I had spoken to did indeed suffer from both scoliosis and had one leg that was literally shorter than the other, rather than because of some misalignment. Of course, I had no idea at all. She asked if I would be prepared to minister to the other lady. Naturally, I said I would, if she was willing for that to happen.

So, later in the afternoon, *Delia* brought *Madeleine* over to meet me. She was happy to receive ministry but was clearly very nervous. Delia helped me (part of our strategy to get others involved) and all three of us saw the short leg grow out very quickly. Madeleine stood up and immediately noticed the difference. Then we ministered to her back. She was aware that God was doing something, but she would need to check it out at home later.

The next day Madeleine testified at the healing service about her leg and said that she was still not sure if her spine had straightened but the pain level was reduced considerably. Cathy and I saw her again a couple of weeks later and, although her testimony was still valid, we could see that her back was still at least slightly out of alignment and so we offered to pray again. We prayed for that need, and in response to another request she made, and then saw quite clearly that her back was now straight. God is so good!

NOTES

[1] A name given in italics at first mention is not the person's real name and is used for reasons of confidentiality.

[2] Mark Marx has written a very good book (*Stepping into the Impossible*, River Publishing, 2015) telling his own story and explaining how the HoTS ministry came about.

[3] Chapter 5 in Roberts Liardon's book, *God's Generals: The Healing Evangelists*, tells the story of Charles and Frances Hunter, known as the Happy Hunters. I recommend it to you for your encouragement.

[4] Arnold Muwonge is the overseer of Destiny Bridge churches in Uganda. He is the founder and director of NDE Network, a ministry dedicated to discipleship, equipping church leaders and community transformation throughout the world. He leads the Bridge Leadership Network and over the past ten years and more his teaching ministry has impacted many Western churches, especially in Europe. He is also the director of Kampala Children's Home, which is the home of Destiny Africa Children's Choir.

[5] Paul Bennison, an Englishman currently based in Northern Ireland, has been an itinerant missionary since 1988, and has visited many nations preaching the gospel, seeing the sick healed and the dead raised, teaching in Bible schools, working alongside churches, and helping with aid, relief and development on an individual and corporate level in many countries in the developing world. He has a special affinity for the city of Cali in Colombia and, at the time of writing, we have just returned from a visit to Cali with him, during which we saw many people healed and set free.

■

Chapter 3

WORDS OF KNOWLEDGE[1]

To one there is given through the Spirit ...
the message [or word] of knowledge.

(1 Corinthians 12:8b, NIV 1984)

BACK IN FEBRUARY 2011, WHEN EAGLES 4031 was little more than an eaglet peering over the edge of an eyrie, we were invited to go to a church in Essex for a healing service on a Sunday morning. This was to be followed by healing workshops in the afternoon. Hindsight reveals that this was the first trial run of what our ministry would turn out to be. Before leaving home, I remember saying to Cathy, 'We have only met three people from that church, we are doing the service before the workshops (instead of, ideally, the other way around) and the good people of Romford are going to expect something to happen, in the context of healing, by the end of the meeting.' We felt that the best thing would be to ask the Lord for words of knowledge (for ailments) to share at a suitable time during the morning, so we did.

God was gracious to us and we wrote down four or five 'words', as we believe we received them from Holy Spirit. One of these was more of an encouraging 'paragraph', a short message rather than a single word, and the others related to various conditions. The most alarming one (we had not yet grasped that, with God and His healing, there are *no* degrees of difficulty between different ailments) was 'cerebral palsy'. Towards the end of the morning meeting, we shared all the words and each one was responded to by at least one person. And that 'alarming' word was claimed by someone who lived next door to a young man who suffered from cerebral palsy. He really wanted to reach out to his neighbour with the love of God. Our *Abba* is such an encourager, isn't He?

The sick people were all prayed for and, as far as I can recall, each received at least a measure of healing. We deemed the workshop to be successful, as our wish to involve the congregation in ministering to one another was fulfilled and several healings took place. I recall vividly that, at one point, we had a line of perhaps half a dozen people, all with back trouble, with another line of people standing behind ministering healing to them.

We were so encouraged that we felt sure we must be on the path the Lord was setting out ahead of us. This was sort of 'confirmed', in a contrary way, by the fact that we were subjected to a demonic attack in the car on the way home. First, our new satnav tried to send us the wrong way after we had reached a familiar part of the route home. Now I know satnavs can do that at times, without any outside help, but then I began to feel like something was trying to obstruct my vision of the road ahead. It was like what happens when someone comes up behind you and puts their hands over your eyes! We were nearly forced off the road before we expelled it – in Jesus' name. There will be more about 'opposition' in another chapter.

What is a word of knowledge? The following is probably the best definition I have come across thus far: 'A word of knowledge is a supernatural revelation of information by the Holy Spirit. It is not something that the person who receives it can know through his or her own natural senses.'

I hope those readers who are already familiar with this gift will forgive me if I focus my attention upon those who have not been similarly enlightened previously. Anyway, I trust everyone will agree that it is good for each of us to be reminded occasionally of what we already know (see 2 Peter 1:12).

Healing is the primary focus of this book, so it is important to emphasise that words of knowledge are not exclusively received and shared in the context of the healing ministry. However, for our present purposes, we will mostly concentrate on Holy Spirit giving the revelatory gift of a word of knowledge concerning a person's need for healing, which can also include a need to be set free from demonic influence or oppression.

Probably the most common use of this gift is to reveal certain conditions that may be present in the room as an indication of the desire of God to heal or set free the person or persons affected by those conditions. However, it is also used by God to bring additional information during a time of ministry. For example, He may use it to achieve breakthrough when there seems to be some sort of obstruction to healing or to the progress of the ministry.

The revelation of a word of knowledge builds faith for ministry, particularly for the person ministering, although this can be equally true for the person being ministered to, whether they are Christian or not. Faith is an important component of the healing ministry, but God is sovereign, so I would hesitate to apply that as a 'rule'.

There are plenty of testimonies of healing where little or no faith has been expressed by anyone!

Bill Johnson, senior pastor of Bethel Church, Redding, California, says that, 'God never contradicts His Word, but He has no problem with contradicting our understanding of His Word.' So, rule number one of this ministry is never to set any rules or rely on formulae based on experiences to date. It is much better – and much wiser – to listen for Holy Spirit's prompting *every* time you minister. He does not always do things in the same way He did them the last time. Just look at how the Gospels record the different ways Jesus healed the blind or leprous. God's creativity knows no bounds.

Anyone can receive a word of knowledge from Holy Spirit. If there is any prerequisite at all, it is to have the desire to be used by God in this way. It is another one of those areas in the Christian life where we should push past our fears and step out boldly as He leads us. After all, if we expect nothing, we are not likely to be disappointed! A good and safe place to learn and to experiment is in a small group of like-minded people intent on helping and encouraging one another. This is the ideal environment in which to make our inevitable initial mistakes as we seek to experience more of the goodness of God.

Back in 1984, Randy Clark was introduced to **five** different ways by which a word of knowledge can be received.[2] Over the next 30 plus years he has added **two** more from his own experience, so it is these **seven** different ways that I want us to look at individually now.

Of course, it is certainly not very wise to say that there are *only* these seven different expressions, either now or in the future. However, they do form a broad base that will be sufficient for most people in ministry, unless or until they receive a new and different form of revelation.

FEEL IT

You feel a word of knowledge when you actually experience a physical, sympathetic pain in your body, which you know is not your own pain. It may only last for a second or three, so, if you have no expectation that Holy Spirit works in this way, you can easily miss it.

This is how Randy Clark has had the most experience of receiving words of knowledge over the years. However, with *tempus 'fugitting'* relentlessly, it is very possible that it will become the least reliable for any of us, the more we advance in years and begin to creak a bit as a result!

I can remember being part of the ministry team when our home church held a healing conference for health professionals that ran alongside our Healing Centre. The delegates, not all of whom were necessarily Christians, were invited to join us for worship before the Healing Centre opened to the public. During this time, the team members were released to minister a blessing to any delegates who were happy for that to happen.

Connor and I approached a lady and asked if we could bless her. She agreed and, as we prayed blessing over her, I felt a very sharp pain in my lower back. I asked her if she had such a pain and she said she had. She was happy for us to minister healing and, while we were doing this, I felt the pain even more sharply for a second or two before it disappeared completely.

We asked her how she was feeling, and she said the pain had completely gone – praise God! I then stuck my neck out and asked her if, before it disappeared, it had suddenly got worse. She said that indeed it had! So, on this occasion, I had felt the word of knowledge twice (which I assume is rare).

READ IT

This is the type of word of knowledge that has been most common in my own experience. You will 'see' words in your mind's eye. For some people, it is like reading a big newspaper headline. For others, it looks more like a ticker tape moving by. I have occasionally seen a word or words lit up like a neon sign. Sometimes these words are seen 'on' or 'over' a person, which can make it more obvious that he or she is the intended recipient of the message.

I remember meeting my friend, Clive, in a large shopping centre where he is a part-time chaplain to the staff. He had come off duty and, after having lunch together, we were going to pray and then wander around the building to see if God had any divine appointments lined up for us. Clive did say that he had a booklet to deliver to a girl who was an assistant in one of 'his' shops first, as he had not had time to do that in the morning. So, we headed for that shop and I waited by the entrance while Clive went in to speak to the two young women working there.

While he was chatting, I saw the word 'headache' hovering in the air inside the shop in two different places, both near to where the girls were standing. As this was happening, it transpired that Clive had been talking about God healing today and had asked if either of them had pain in their bodies. One girl said she had, and was happy for us to pray with her, so we all went into the storeroom at the back of the shop so as not to alarm any customers!

She had intermittent pain in her back and knee but was not experiencing any discomfort at that moment. Nevertheless, we prayed for her, realising that we would not be able to know straight away what the result would be. We then prayed for and prophesied over her colleague before introducing what I had perceived earlier.

I asked the girls if either of them had a headache. One said she had suffered one yesterday but was pain free today. The other said she had one the day before that but she was OK now.

Shortly afterwards a friend of theirs, who worked in another store, came into the room. I think the three young women were going to have a late lunch together. After exchanging pleasantries, Clive explained what we had just been doing, so I took a 'risk' and asked the third girl if, by any chance, she was suffering with a headache. She was, and it was quite a severe one!

She was happy for us to minister to her and, as we were about to do so, I 'read' the word 'stress' and asked her if her headache was stress-related. 'Tell me about it!' she said. 'Family issues, work issues!' So, we prayed briefly and commanded the stress to be lifted off her and for the pain to go. She declared that she was instantly pain free!

A short while ago, just before we were to go on holiday, I had to replace my wireless printer. I spent an unexpectedly and inexplicably fruitless time trying to get this connected to my computer. After a few hours, I gave up and went for a long, hot soak in the bath to wash away the stress. Lying among the bubbles, I suddenly saw in my mind's eye the name of a WiFi connection which was a generic BT one rather than the identity of our own hub/router thingy (no, I am not a techie!). I had seen this earlier on my computer, but it had not registered with me in a helpful way. Immediately, I realised what the problem was. My computer had picked up the wrong WiFi source, so it was conflicting with the correct source the new printer had picked up. The following morning, bright and early, I installed the printer very quickly!

SEE IT

'I have a picture of [whatever it may be]. Does this mean anything to you?' This question, or something very much like it, has been asked in the church circles I have moved in for the past 30 years or so. I am referring to mental pictures, something you *see* in your mind's eye. Yes, it is the imagination at work but, as Christians, we can justifiably claim to have a sanctified imagination when God chooses to communicate with and through us in this way (see 1 Corinthians 2:16b).

I remember being in a youth service at our previous home church. The young people were doing most of the 'upfront' stuff. Two girls were leading the meeting between them. Part way through, I saw, in my mind's eye, a picture of a young lady from the lower back view. All I could see was that she was wearing tight, pale-coloured trousers and dark 'pixie' boots. There was an arrow, just as you might find in a diagram, pointing towards one of her feet. I interpreted this to mean that there was a problem with that foot or ankle. I sought and was given permission to share this word at the end of the meeting and, as I did so, I suddenly heard myself saying something unplanned: 'No, I believe she has one leg shorter than the other.' (More later about saying something 'unplanned' like that.)

Cathy and I waited around for several minutes at the end of the meeting to see if anyone would respond to the word by going forward to the ministry team on duty that morning, but nobody did. Thinking that it is not possible to be accurate every time, we started to make our way towards the back of the church and the exit. As we did so, a teenage girl came through the doors and headed towards the side aisle of the building. Somehow, I 'knew' that was her and went back to the ministry team leader to report this. I was asked to go and pray with the girl, and the leader sent *Karen*, a female member of the team, to accompany me. I think Cathy must have been called away by someone, otherwise she would have gone with me.

As we approached the girl, I realised she had been one of those leading the service and asked her if she had not heard the 'word of knowledge' I gave out at the end of the meeting. 'No,' she said, 'by then I must have gone out to the kitchen to help with the coffees.' I explained what the word was and pointed out that she was wearing the same sort of trousers that I had seen, although she was shoeless. She told us that she had come to church wearing pixie boots, but she had taken them off much earlier on!

Then I noticed that she was standing with her feet slightly turned inwards (or it may have been outwards). I mentioned this to her and said that it can sometimes mean that there is pelvic misalignment. She let us pray for that, with Karen laying hands on her hips, and she went into 'hula-hoop' mode as God made some minor adjustments to her stance. Then we returned to the 'real' reason for approaching her. She said she was not aware of having one leg shorter than the other but was happy for us to pray for her in case she had.

We sat her down and Karen took the girl's feet in her hands. It was immediately obvious that there was a slight difference between the apparent lengths of her legs. So we prayed, commanding the 'short' leg to grow out, and Karen let out a squeal of delighted surprise as it quickly and clearly grew out in her hands as she watched!

We spoke to the girl's mother shortly afterwards, to explain what had happened, and she said she had no idea that her daughter had one leg shorter than the other, although she had often com-plained about backaches. I informed Mum that she wouldn't be doing that any more! God is so good!

THINK IT

This kind of word of knowledge comes as a thought or an impres-sion or a knowing that suddenly 'lands' in your mind. With practice, you get to tell the difference between a thought that is your own and one that is planted in your mind by Holy Spirit. The enemy will always tempt you to think that you just made it up yourself, so I suggest you always speak it out to check if it is just you or not. This can be done in a simple, humble way without any hype or embarrassment.

This is the type of 'word' that Cathy is inclined to receive most of the time. It usually comes to her while she is already ministering to someone and often serves as a revelation which overcomes an obstacle in the healing process or a bit of reluctance by the 'client' to be completely open and trusting. I also mentioned my experience of 'knowing' in the previous example, when I just knew who my word was for when the girl walked back into the room.

As with all possible God-given words of knowledge, the only way to find out for certain if they are from Him or not is to have the boldness to speak them out. If this is done gently, then it is no big deal if they prove to be just your own thoughts. The other thing to remember with words of knowledge is that, just because nobody responds, it does not mean that you did not hear accurately from Holy Spirit. We have lost count of the number of times someone has come out at the end of a meeting, after most people have gone home, and admitted, 'Sorry I didn't respond before, but that was for me.'

I was involved, as an ESSL[3] student, in another conference, this one for leadership teams from a variety of churches, both in the UK and further afield in Europe. Again, we were released to minister to receptive delegates during the worship time that opened the meeting. I was standing near a lady when a strange thought came into my head. I was suddenly aware of the story title, 'The Tortoise and the Hare'. I was quite sure that it was for this woman but, as it was so strange, it took me a few moments to remind myself that I had nothing to lose by testing it out as a word of knowledge.

When I approached her to introduce myself, I noticed, from her delegate badge, that she was from the Faroe Islands. It was also quickly obvious that her English was better than mine! She told me she was familiar with the story and only then did I receive and deliver a prophetic word for her that drew on that fable. When I asked her if what I had spoken out made any sense, her exact reply was that it was 'spot on' and described her situation accurately! This was not a healing encounter, but I use it as an illustration of the 'unusual'.

SAY IT

Probably the best way to describe this variety of word of knowledge is as 'inspired speech'. This is another one that is more likely to come up during a time of ministry rather than beforehand. You simply find yourself saying something that you had not meant or planned to say, before you said it, but it proves to be the very word or phrase that is needed to move the ministry on at that point. You could say that it is rather like speaking in tongues in that the cognitive part of the mind is temporarily bypassed.

An example of this would be when I spoke out about the mental picture I had seen of the girl with the trousers and pixie boots with an arrow pointing to her foot. I intended to say that I believed she had a damaged foot or ankle but heard myself correcting that to say, 'No, she has one leg shorter than the other.' The definitive statement was spoken out without me ever thinking those words, let alone planning to say them.

On another occasion, as an ESSL student, I was with a group on the streets of Gravesend. Our team was manning the gazebo we had set up in the pedestrianised street. *James* and I were on prophetic appointments duty. A young lady approached our table, which had various photographs on it, and we invited her to choose one that 'stood out' to her. She did that, and we duly prophesied over her from what we believed Holy Spirit was saying through the photograph. This led to healing ministry for a trapped nerve, but that is not the point of this example.

As we were talking to her, sharing the love of God, I suddenly found myself saying, 'You are not an accident, you know.' She responded, 'But I have always thought that I was.' She went on to explain that her mother died giving birth to her and that her father died when she was still a little girl. In addition to that, her parents were not married, so she had not been 'planned'. James shared with her how much her heavenly Father loved her and that, to Him, she was not an 'accident' but a very precious daughter. She was speechless with wonder. Have I mentioned how good God is?!

Well, that concludes the **five** ways of receiving words of knowledge that Randy Clark found out about during his telephone conversation with Lance Pittock all those years ago. Cathy and I can claim to have experienced each of these at least once although, in my case, the most common way is to read it and for Cathy it is to think/know it. Now we move on to the additional **two**, although I must be honest and say that neither of us has knowingly experienced either of them personally (yet).

DREAM IT

This one is self-explanatory but, to be fair, most of us do not have an opportunity to sleep and dream either immediately before or during a meeting! How it usually works is for the person to dream about something and, in a subsequent ministry situation, God brings the dream to mind and they have the faith to speak it out and act upon it at that time.

For instance, Randy Clark shares about a man who dreamed that he was out driving in his car in an area he did not recognise and, as he approached a sharp bend, he felt a strong impression that he should pull off the road. With a little reluctance, he gave heed to the impression and pulled over. Just after he did so, another car sped around the bend on the wrong side of the road to overtake a lorry! The evasive action, taken before he understood the pressing need to do so, avoided a head-on collision that would probably have proved fatal.

Sometime later the same man was driving his car in a region he was not familiar with and suddenly recognised the road with the dangerous bend that he had seen in his dream. He got the same strong impression to pull off the road and, immediately after he had done so ... well, you can guess the rest. The dream proved to be a word of knowledge that saved lives!

This is a good example of what I said earlier: words of knowledge are by no means confined to the healing ministry – although you might identify this case as an example of pre-ventative care! God loves us and is concerned about healing and protecting the whole person. He longs to bring health and freedom in all circumstances.

EXPERIENCE IT

This one is probably the most difficult to put into words, especially for someone who has no personal examples to illustrate it with (although a corporate one is included below). Nevertheless, it seems right to include both 'additional' ways because Holy Spirit may choose to communicate with you by means of one or both and you may not already be aware of these possibilities.

Randy Clark gives, as one example, the time his wife was making a telephone call and it appears she got a crossed line (remember those?) that would not clear. She heard a couple who were having a conversation in which they were planning an illicit liaison. Deanne forgot all about it until, during a church meeting some while later, God brought it back to her mind.

She shared this, carefully and tactfully, as a word of knowledge relating to adultery. A young man told her after the meeting that he had been making such a telephone call, the purpose of which had been to set up an adulterous relationship. He repented, and the problem was averted, no doubt saving much heartache.

So, it is possible that Holy Spirit will communicate with us even through some strange or bizarre experience to bring someone into healing, to set them free or to rescue them from something untoward. Let us not limit Him to whatever our experiences have been to date. He is *big*. He is sovereign. He is creative. He can do or use anything He wants to communicate with us.

Finally, let's look at the corporate example I mentioned earlier. This was at the beginning of my first term at ESSL (day school). At the time, the access road to Eastgate came to a dead end just after a right-angle bend past our church car park. (That is no longer the case as Ebbsfleet Garden City is being built around us as I write!) Anyway, a large articulated lorry had obviously driven round the bend to the dead end and the driver was struggling to reverse his way back out to the main road again. The point of the story is that the lorry had emblazoned on the sides the message 'Hell's Energy Drink' and the strapline 'Gives you the power of hell!' The lorry was spotted during our powerful worship time and the interpretation of the experience was that 'hell retreats as we worship'! Hallelujah – what an encouragement!

SHARING WORDS

A word or message of knowledge is a gift of Holy Spirit and, just like a word of prophecy, it is intended for edification and/or for building up the Body of Christ, if not for healing (see 1 Corinthians 14:3).

You and I will get it wrong sometimes. Let's go for it again anyway. The more we are emboldened to share what we believe we have received, the more easily we will recognise when we have heard from God and the more accurate we will become. It is a progressive thing and, just like any other activity, our level of expertise will only increase with experience. It is like exercising the muscles of our body. Some people suggest that we have a 'faith muscle' that needs to be exercised and built up. James 2:26 reminds us that faith is not really faith until it involves *doing* something, putting theory into practice.

Faith is exercised through obedience and a willingness to risk. The late John Wimber actually taught that 'faith' is spelt: R.I.S.K. Faith is having the confidence to step out in the first place, rather than being focused only on the intended result of so doing. It is important to be willing to step out of our comfort zones because this can bring freedom to those we minister to. With that goal in mind it is worth the risk of possibly making ourselves look a little foolish. Most people, especially non-Christians it seems, will appreciate that we care for them enough to take a chance.

We must be careful how we share these words with people, whether in a corporate meeting or in a one-to-one situation. It is important that we act with love and humility. Even if we feel 100% certain we have heard from the Lord it is still possible that we could be wrong, so let us be careful that our assumption does not turn out to be presumption. Instead, try to deliver a word in such a way that neither party will have cause to be embarrassed or offended, whether it proves to be accurate or not. Reading 1 Corinthians 13:9 reminds us that, for now, each one of us knows only in part, no matter how experienced or confident we may be.

If we deliver our words too authoritatively and they prove not to be accurate, they could have a very negative impact upon the recipient, pushing them into unhealthy introspection or maybe even putting them under unnecessary condemnation. And do, please, be ultra-careful when personal issues are involved, realising that sometimes the revelation is for information only, intended to prompt prayer but not to be spoken out, especially through a microphone in a corporate setting.

An important thing to resist is the temptation to embellish what we have received from Holy Spirit. Deliver what you get and don't add to it for any reason. Randy Clark provides an example of a situation where he delivered a word of knowledge about someone falling over a hose. He was convinced that the word was an accurate one, but it was not responded to until he persisted out of his firm conviction. A man who had injured himself in such circumstances finally acknowledged that the word was for him, but he had hesitated to respond because Randy had said the hose was green and he had tripped over a yellow one at an airport. Randy apologised for including the word 'green' in the delivery. It was not what he had seen or heard. He mentioned it simply because he was familiar only with green (garden) hoses!

When sharing words of knowledge, we will do well to avoid hype, unnatural pseudo-spiritual language or attitudes, overuse of authority and 'Christianese' (i.e. churchy jargon that any non-Christians present would not understand). Normal, everyday language really is all that is called for, just being naturally supernatural, like Jesus.

Can I suggest that you share words of knowledge using phrases like the following but, obviously, in your own words and not as though following a script you have learned?

- 'I am not sure, but I think that the Lord may be saying to [telling] me that [this and that].'
- 'Is it possible that the word [whatever it may be] means something to you?'

- 'I am sensing [such and such] and wonder if this resonates with you at all?'

The well-known prophetic minister, Shawn Bolz, has an excellent way of dealing with an absence of a response. He just says something like, 'Sorry, I am practising hearing from God and sometimes I get it wrong.' He tells of one occasion when this happened to him and the person he spoke to was so intrigued that someone would claim to hear from God that he initiated a conversation which ended with Shawn leading him to Christ! By the way, if you are familiar with Shawn's ministry you will know how detailed and incredibly accurate the revelatory words he receives can be.

If all this is new to you then I recommend again that you learn, practise and make your initial mistakes in a small group of like-minded people providing a safe environment within which the primary aim is to encourage one another. Remember, words of knowledge are not exclusively for apostles, prophets, evangelists, pastors or teachers but for *every* member of the Body of Christ. That includes children, because there is no 'Junior' Holy Spirit! God can and does use the very young and they have the advantage of being much more open and less inhibited than most adults – especially, dare I say it, we British!

Cathy and I recently had a 5-year-old boy share some amazingly encouraging words with us. Also, I was part of an ESSL Equipping Team visiting another church where children were actively involved in much of what we did, and their 'words' were often more accurate than those of the adults!

Remember also that you can receive these words anywhere, not just in a church service or small group meetings. You will recall that I shared with you earlier what I 'read' in a large shopping centre. Words of knowledge are an excellent tool for evangelism, especially when coupled with the prophetic and/or healing. You

may recall that John Wimber wrote a book called *Power Evangelism*
and today we have ministries like Treasure Hunting[4] that put power
evangelism into practice.

Other outreach ministries like Healing on the Streets and
Healing Rooms utilise words of knowledge on a regular basis. If you
are serious about the healing ministry, why don't you 'Google' to
see if one of these operates in your area and, if so, join in. If not,
you could organise a 'treasure hunt' with like-minded friends. Or
just go out on the street or down to the beach, asking the Lord to
set up divine appointments with opportunities to receive and share
words of knowledge for healing and/or for prophecy.

You will be co-operating with and bringing an answer to that
part of the Lord's Prayer that says, 'Your Kingdom come, your
will be done, on earth as it is in heaven.'

NOTES

[1] The content of this chapter owes much to the teaching of Randy Clark of
Global Awakening Ministries and his publication *Words of Knowledge* (Kindle
edition, 2011), for which I am most grateful.

[2] This was in a telephone conversation many years ago between Randy Clark
and Lance Pittock, a pastor at the Anaheim Vineyard church in California.

[3] See Chapter 4 for more about the Eastgate School of Supernatural Life.

[4] Read *The Ultimate Treasure Hunt* by Kevin Dedmon (Destiny Image, 2007)
for more detailed information.

■

Chapter 4

THE THREE 'I'S: IDENTITY + INTIMACY = IMPACT¹

*Jesus knew that the Father had put all things under his power,
and that he had come from God and was returning to God; so he ...
began to wash his disciples' feet ...*

(John 13:3–5)

IT WAS BACK IN SEPTEMBER 2010 that Cathy and I
started attending the School of Supernatural Ministry run by
North Kent Community Church, now known as Eastgate,
which has been our home church¹ since June 2015. The course
lasted for two years of three terms each and we met every other
Wednesday evening for two hours (or so!). The first hour involved
worship, testimonies and announcements. The second majored
on teaching, with the sessions becoming more interactive in the
second year.

The school was a wonderful experience for Cathy and me. It helped us to grow and to appreciate that 'there is always more' of the infinite and eternal Kingdom of God. The Bethel School (Redding, California) was the model and more churches are starting similar schools as time goes by.

There was great emphasis placed on the Three 'I's and the way they are interlinked: Identity + Intimacy = Impact. The bottom line is that, the more you know who you are in Christ (Identity) and the deeper you go in your relationship with Father (Intimacy), the greater will be the effect that you have on the community around you as you live out what is being built into your life by Holy Spirit (Impact). This was the firm foundation on which the school curriculum was based. We loved it and we absorbed it as best we could. We seek to live it out, both inside and outside church. The best thing of all is that this is for every Christian.

The evening school is still going strong and operates in tandem with a daytime school. It is now known as the Eastgate School of Supernatural Life (ESSL). In fact, I signed up for the 'day school', which runs for two full days each week, for the 2016–17 academic year, then for a further academic year. I was finally able to dismiss thoughts of being too old for this when I met an 84-year-old lady who had just completed her two years and is herself a glowing endorsement for the school, as she demonstrated in a promotional video for ESSL released in 2016!

There is no shortage in the numbers of students wanting to be involved each year and they come from pretty much all over the place. In my first year of day school my fellow students were from many parts of the UK, seven from France, one each from Switzerland and the Faroe Islands, and a married couple all the way from Kenya!

So, there must be something fundamentally essential for the fruitful Christian life in the Three 'I's principle, something we all need to tap into for the ultimate blessing of those we meet. For this reason, Cathy and I have unashamedly 'pinched' all we can from what we have learned, to pass it on in our Eagles 4031 workshops. (Well, Eastgate took most of it from Bethel, and Holy Spirit provided the revelation and inspiration for both of them.)

IDENTITY

When we are born again (John 3:3) we become a brand-new creation (2 Corinthians 5:17) and we take on a new, spiritual identity. From that moment on we are adopted children of God, members of the royal family of Heaven, partners in the family business. But is it always in that wonderful context that we live our new lives?

Are we aware of, or do we even understand, all that is available to us? How many of us, as babes in Christ, are taught these things? It is only in the more recent years of my own life that my eyes and heart have been increasingly opened to what God has made available for me (and each one of us). So much has been made possible and experiential through obtaining a greater and more accurate appreciation of my identity in Christ.

I once did a Google search for a definition of 'identity' and came up with the following. If I say that I have never heard it put so simply, I trust you will appreciate that my tongue is firmly in my cheek. However, it may well appeal to those of a more intellectual bent than me!

A person's IDENTITY is defined as the totality of one's self-construal, in which how one construes oneself in the present expresses the continuity between how one construes oneself as one was in the past and how one construes oneself as one aspires to be in the future.

(Weinreich)

My preference would be to begin with an appreciation that each individual God has created is as unique as a fingerprint. No two of us ever have been, nor ever will be, exactly alike. What is important is how we see ourselves, especially if that does not correspond with how our Creator sees us. Even though each Christian is a new creation and the old has gone and the new has come (2 Corinthians 5:17), many of us are still labouring under the misapprehension that we are not good enough, that we are somehow unworthy. Given all that Jesus Christ has done for us sacrificially to *make* us worthy, this really smacks of the false humility of a Uriah Heep clone!

How many Christians still view themselves as nasty little worms just about escaping hell by the skin of their teeth? Even *one* of us like that is one too many but, sadly, this is something that it is still taught (and accepted without question) from some church pulpits. In our desperate desire to avoid falling victim to pride we tend to go to the other extreme and, in so doing, it is invariably the false version of humility that we end up expressing.

There is a big difference between confidence and arrogance and we should not confuse the two. Confidence means living out of our true identity. Arrogance is living out of the desire to appear confident. Confident people unsettle insecure people, and the latter accuse the former of arrogance. I remember David Webster teaching us at ESSL that true humility is knowing how great you are (in Jesus). Just take a few moments to absorb that truth.

By the grace of God, no matter how or what we were before we met Him, all is different now. God sees us as He made us to be. In Christ, each of us is the finished article, each one is seated with Him in the heavenly places (Ephesians 2:6), a chosen people, a royal priesthood, a holy nation (1 Peter 2:9). I believe that, in Christ, our position changes immediately we are born again but, in daily life, we are a work in progress, developing towards maturity (2 Peter 1:3–7).

Thanks to the amazing grace of God we are so privileged, for in Christ:

- I am accepted
- I am secure
- I am significant

There is a whole raft of scriptures I could quote here, if space permitted, to support these three declarations. As it is, I am sure that you will already know many of them and not need further convincing from the Word of God.

I am a *son* of the living God, adopted into His family (Romans 8:15) but do I still live as a *servant*, not knowing my Father's business (John 15:15)? The parable of the prodigal son shows us what a contrast there is between these two perceptions or attitudes. It also highlights just how the Father sees us and longs for us to appreciate our inheritance as His sons. (Sorry, ladies, but you know that the word 'sons' includes you just as the term 'the Bride of Christ' includes men!)

The prodigal proved to be a wastrel and went off to squander his inheritance in ways that he knew would grieve his loving father. Eventually he saw the error of his ways and returned to his father, happy to be treated as a servant because even his father's servants had a better lifestyle than the one he had descended into. But his father welcomed him back as his son, just as though nothing had happened, and treated him as such. This is amazing **grace**.

The dutiful elder brother remained at home the whole time, diligently working his socks off and not expecting any great reward. After all, if he had received all his father considered him entitled to (he had also received his share of the inheritance, remember) he would not have been able to justify his superior attitude to his sinful younger brother. What was his father's response to the elder son's assertion that he had never been given a fatted calf for a feast with his friends? He said, in effect, 'Never mind about just a fatted calf – the whole farm is yours!' This is also amazing **grace**.

The prodigal felt that, despite his genuine repentance, it was enough for him to be a servant rather than the son his father welcomed him back as. The elder brother had done nothing to compromise his entitlements as a son, but he viewed everything from the position of a servant. They were both in error, as the grace of the father expressed towards each of them made very clear.

Just how aware are you that you are a son or daughter of the living God, the heavenly Father, with an entitlement to everything that the Lord Jesus Christ has paid the price for you to receive by grace?

It is vital for each one of us to grasp the reality of God's rich provision for us, regardless of whether we think we deserve it or not. The fact is, we don't deserve it, but He gives it to us anyway. He loves us so much, more deeply than we can ever imagine. He is a perfect Daddy, our Abba!

INTIMACY

Intimacy means being in the presence of someone, getting to know his or her heart. This is especially true of those deeper human relationships we have, like marriage or very close friendships. And it is intended to be equally true of our relationship with God: Father, Son and Holy Spirit.

God *loves* us. We are each unique, special and precious to Him and He wants to spend quality time with us. We need to become more intimate with God so that we can know His blessings and become a blessing to others as carriers of His presence wherever we go. The more we allow our focus to be upon Him, the more we will reflect, or re-present, Him when we are with others.

The purpose of intimacy with Jesus is to have a revelation of the Father. If your eyes are not opened to the Father, you have not entered into the fullness of intimacy with Christ.

(David Wilkerson)

Devotion to prayer and intimacy with God is the only setting in which we can completely step into the fullness of God's purposes.

(Bill Johnson)

God sees each of us as a precious treasure, the apple of His eye, and He longs to have a close relationship with us. More than anything, He wants us to have an intimate love relationship and friendship with Him. God wants us to spend time with Him and intimately communicate with Him. To trust and follow Him. To give our lives meaning and purpose by giving us the privilege of joining Him in His work.

You, God, are my God, earnestly I seek you; I thirst for you, my whole being longs for you, in a dry and parched land where there is no water. I have seen you in the sanctuary and beheld your power and your glory. Because your love is better than life, my lips will glorify you. I will praise you as long as I live, and in your name I will lift up my hands. I will be satisfied as with the richest of foods; with singing lips my mouth will praise you. On my bed I remember you; I think of you through the watches of the night.

(Psalm 63:1–6)

As our relationship with God becomes more intimate, so our confidence to be able to hear the voice of God for ourselves will grow. We will gradually become less dependent upon hearing from Him only through someone like a famous preacher or an established church leader.

Cathy is, by nature, a bit of a 'Martha' but she is learning to be more of a 'Mary' (see Luke 10:38–42). During one of her quiet times with God He shared with her that He wanted her to 'be busy from a place of rest'. That really is the key to ministry of any kind. Bill Johnson teaches that faith is not effort but surrender. This means that we can be active from a place of rest in Him.

Like Mary, it is important to prioritise being with Him, in His presence, over general busy-ness. Some of us too easily fall into the trap of believing that what we *do* is of more importance to God than the time we spend with Him *before* we do anything and our conscious awareness of His presence *while* we are doing it. A perfect example of this is Brother Lawrence who practised the presence of God while going about his menial work in the kitchen.

John Wesley would get up at 4am each day for prayer, spending time in the Father's presence, before embarking on the invariably heavy workload ahead of him. Spending time in His presence first ensures that His presence is carried, with awareness, with us for the rest of the day.

> I am the vine; you are the branches. If you remain in me and I in you, you will bear much fruit; **apart** from me you can do nothing.

> (John 15:5)

IMPACT

If I know who I am in Christ and my relationship with Father is growing in intimacy, then I am making good progress in the process of sanctification, which is the purpose of Holy Spirit for us in this life and to which His activity on our behalf is concentrated

(1 Thessalonians 5:23). This means that I am becoming more like Him, making it seem only naturally supernatural to do the things Jesus did.

Do I really need to remind you about John 14:12 (our call to do the works of Jesus)? When we do these things then, inevitably, we will have some sort of impact upon family, friends and the community around us. In using the word 'we' I am not forgetting that these good things happen only in co-operation with and dependence upon Holy Spirit.

What should I *do*? That can be summed up very easily in a few words. Be bold – and go! Take courage and step out into the gifts of the Spirit. Understand that your activities do not need to be confined within the four walls of a church building. Jesus went where the people were and, sadly, only a comparatively small percentage of the UK population can be found attending church.

People like Fox, Wesley and Whitfield were barred from ministering in many church buildings, so they went out into the highways and byways, exactly where the people were waiting for them, even if those people did not always know that was what they were doing!

What do I *need*? I need to know who I am in Christ, to be secure in my **identity**. I need to remember that I am accepted, secure and significant – in Christ. Through my growing **intimacy** with God I need to become ever more aware that I am loved as a son or daughter, a partner in the family business. I have direct access to the Father through Jesus by Holy Spirit.

Of course, an increasing knowledge of the Word of God will be invaluable. I do not mean by this a knowledge dependent solely upon intellect but also upon wisdom, revelation and experience. Kris Vallotton encourages us to learn to know the Prince over and above the Principles.

If I find myself questioning whether I have enough faith, I should remind myself just how small a mustard seed is (see Matthew 13:31–32). The key to faith is whom it is invested in, not how much of it we think we have. In the final analysis, faith is a gift, not something we work up. I would reiterate that it is not about our effort but our surrender – to Him. It helps to be familiar with the will of God, summed up beautifully in the phrase from the Lord's Prayer, 'on earth as it is in heaven'. For example, there is no sickness in Heaven.

Where do I *go*? We always have two options at any given moment. We can either step forward in faith, spelled R.I.S.K., or we can step back into safety, what we usually call our 'comfort zone'. Look to keep moving forward because it is easy to stop and simply exchange one comfort zone for another.

Begin within the church building or where you meet with like-minded brothers and sisters in a home-group type of environment. Then step outside of the church boundaries into the wider world, where the need is great. Healing for the non-Christian is a reminder that it is the kindness of God that leads to repentance (Romans 2:4).

You can get involved with Treasure Hunts, Healing on the Streets, Healing Rooms or with friends, family or strangers in any environment. Wherever you go you carry the presence of God with you. As you continue to 'be being filled', He expects you to leak, to overflow!

So just go and keep your spiritual eyes and ears open for the prompting of Holy Spirit into divine appointments, often when and where you least expect them. Through you He wants to make an **impact** in your community, so just be bold and co-operate with Him. Please.

Let me close this chapter with one final reminder of this very simple but profound little sum: Identity + Intimacy = Impact.

NOTES

[1] All the references in this book to Eastgate as our 'home church' are correct at the time of writing but, as you read this, we expect to have completed our house move from Kent to Norfolk and embarked on a new set of Kingdom adventures from there.

■

Chapter 5

HEAVEN'S HEALTH MANIFESTO

Praise the LORD, O my soul, and forget not all his benefits – who forgives all your sins and heals all your diseases.

(Psalm 103:2–3)

IT IS NOT UNUSUAL TO THINK of the ministry of healing as being primarily a New Testament concept, but that is far from the truth as the above, and other, Old Testament passages demonstrate. Indeed, because God is both infinite and eternal, our theology, our knowledge of Him, can never be complete. I am inclined to agree with those who say He cannot even be contained within the pages of His Book (although He will never contradict what we can discover about Him in His written Word).

In considering the above scripture, it is vitally important that first we gain an appreciation of what are all the benefits that the Lord graciously makes available to those who know Him. Then we can go on to concern ourselves with not forgetting any of them, as the psalmist urges. Sorry to labour the point but, sadly, this just does not happen in every church congregation. As a result, many of us miss out on so much, as do those whom the Lord would love to bless through us.

FORGIVENESS

We read in Psalm 103, verse 3, that the Lord forgives all our iniquities. And, as Christians, we know that He has dealt with our sins through the substitutionary death of Jesus on the cross. Every church that preaches the gospel makes this benefit known. The verse then goes on to tell us that He also heals *all* our diseases. Not every church preaches and demonstrates that part of the message. Some may go along with the truths that God can heal and has healed, but not all will endorse the view that He still heals, and that this is in accordance with His perfect will for mankind. But, as I will cover more fully in Chapter 7, the Greek word *sozo*, which is translated into our English Bibles as 'salvation', has a three-fold application, namely forgiveness, healing and deliverance.

HEALING

This *sozo* embraces a major benefit combination of the Kingdom of God. The psalm goes on to give a long list of the Kingdom benefits that are freely available to us but, as our present subject is healing, I do not propose to look at those here, glorious as they are. But it is easy to see that the whole person is intended to benefit in many ways. Healing of our sicknesses, diseases and injuries, both physical and emotional, is simply what I have chosen to concentrate on in this book. In this chapter, we will be looking at principles relating to healing in general; to set down some markers, if you like.

WILLING

My earliest prayers for the sick, and for many other things also, invariably seemed to end with the words, 'if it be Thy will'. Some may consider me to be rather harsh, but I can't help thinking, now, that any prayer that ends like that effectively nullifies any faith that may have been expressed in it beforehand. Ideally, we establish what God's will is in a matter *before* we begin to pray or declare it into being.

There is a teaching principle that whenever something is mentioned in scripture for the first time, it sets a precedent, foundation or guide from which can be based the interpretation of any subsequent mention of that same word or idea. There are many verses in the Old Testament, not just in Psalm 103 (e.g. Exodus 15:26) that show us the will of God regarding sickness or disease. Turning to the New Testament, Mark's Gospel is considered to be the first one to be written and we find him quoting Jesus in his first chapter:

> A man with leprosy came to him and begged him on his knees, 'If you are willing, you can make me clean.' Filled with compassion, Jesus reached out his hand and touched the man. '**I am willing**,' he said. 'Be clean!' Immediately the leprosy left him and he was cured.
>
> (Mark 1:40–41, NIV 1984)

I am absolutely convinced that it is the will of God to heal the sick and, as already quoted from Psalm 103, to heal all our diseases. I confess that not every sick person that I, and others, pray for has obviously been healed there and then. Even so, that does not change my conviction that it is the will of God to heal all the sick of every disease.

You will see that I cover the subject of 'Disappointment' in Chapter 9, and in Chapter 8 I touch on some other issues that might discourage us.

There are two kinds of 'being willing' when it comes to the healing ministry. Believe it or not, some people do not actually *want* to be healed. Many of these still ask for prayer anyway, even if only to gain attention, which is all that some of them really desire.

For some their identity, even a kind of security, is found in their illness and they feel the need to cling to it. To 'own' a disease by calling it '*my* [whatever]' is not a good idea. It can establish a false sense of identity and even operate as a form of self-imposed curse. There is also a sense in which the disease can feed a need for sympathy.

Sometimes there are certain (financial) benefits that will be lost if a sick person is healed. Our good friend, Paul Bennison, had this illustrated when he was ministering in Scandinavia a few years ago.

Paul has been active in the healing ministry for more than 30 years, travelling all over the world. On this occasion he had, if I recall correctly, three men in wheelchairs come out to the front for ministry in a meeting. Paul, as he always does, spent time with each person, learning a little bit of their stories before ministering to them.

The first two were healed and got up out of their wheelchairs. The third guy witnessed all this but, as Paul moved over to pray for him, the man asked, 'If I am healed, does that mean I will lose all my [disability] benefits?' When he was answered in the affirmative, he declined to be prayed for! The man made this choice even though he was married and had young children with whom he was unable to play or to be actively involved in their growing up!

ALL

If we look again at verse 3 we will see that God heals all our diseases. Now it does not matter what language you read this verse in; the equivalent of '*all*' still means all, not *some*! There are no exceptions mentioned. It is not every single one except cancer, or arthritis, or heart disease, or dementia, or anything else you may care to mention. Again, this is shown in scripture and I am just going to quote a couple of typical verses to establish the point:

> When evening came, many who were [demon*ised*][1] were brought to him, and he drove out the spirits with a word and healed **all** who were ill. This was to fulfil what was spoken through the prophet Isaiah: 'He took up our infirmities and bore our diseases.'
>
> (Matthew 8:16–17)

> … Jesus withdrew from that place. A large crowd followed him, and he healed **all** who were ill.
>
> (Matthew 12:15)

EVERY

> Jesus went through all the towns and villages, teaching in their synagogues, proclaiming the good news of the kingdom and healing **every** disease and sickness.
>
> (Matthew 9:35, NIV 1984)

I have no wish to labour the same point made in respect of the word 'all' but, clearly, the same comprehensive meaning also applies to the word 'every'. Scripture shows that Jesus not only healed everyone who came to Him but also that God's grace triumphed over every disease that they brought into His presence. There were no exceptions and John points out that many, many more stories of Jesus' accomplishments could have been recorded.

I will not attempt to deny that also, in this context, you and I will encounter disappointment. Cathy and I have been privileged to witness numerous remarkable healings connected with the skeletal system but none, so far, in respect of some other conditions. But we certainly do not give up. We always press on for new breakthroughs, our target being the 100% 'record' that Jesus had.

Bill Johnson's father died of cancer despite much prayer for healing but, by pressing on through that huge disappointment, he and Bethel Church in general have since seen countless people completely healed from many types of cancer. The Healing Centre attached to Eastgate church is accumulating a growing number of testimonies of cancers being healed, those healings being verified by the medical profession.

One of these was a lady who was operated on ten days after attending the Healing Centre, only for the surgeons to find no trace of cancer in her body. She had a comparatively rare form of the disease, which had taken the life of the mother of one of Eastgate's leaders just nine years before. He had pressed on through that disappointment, with his mother's encouragement to do so.

We have to live with a degree of 'mystery', but breakthrough comes with persistence. Heidi Baker (of Iris Ministries) prayed for very many deaf people without seeing any healing until, at last, the breakthrough came. Now, every time she undertakes pioneer evangelism in a new village in Mozambique, her first cry is 'Bring out your deaf!' and they are healed, often having been prayed for by the children she takes care of in Mozambique and who go on these trips with her.

I have already used the phrase, 'There is no *Junior* Holy Spirit.' He works through male and female, old and young – anyone who is willing to trust Him, to step out in faith and to press in for a breakthrough.

HIS PURPOSE

Luke's Gospel tells us that, after His baptism, Jesus went into the wilderness '**full** of the Holy Spirit', to be subjected to temptations by the devil. When He returned victoriously, we are told that He did so in the '**power** of the Holy Spirit'. So, there is a difference between fullness and power in this context. The fullness, or anointing, that we carry is released in power by *doing*. The time had come for Jesus' ministry to begin and this is how He announced it Himself, quoting from Isaiah 61:

> The Spirit of the Lord is on me, because he has **anointed** me to proclaim good news to the poor. He has sent me to proclaim freedom for the prisoners and recovery of sight for the blind, to set the oppressed free, to proclaim the year of the Lord's favour.
>
> (Luke 4:18–19)

If we wanted to sum up the purpose of the ministry of Jesus in one short sentence, we are not likely to better this one from 1 John 3:8: 'The reason the Son of God appeared was to destroy the devil's work.'

God, in Jesus, has purposed to reconcile the world to Himself (John 3:17). In and through Him, the Kingdom of Heaven invades earth. This is the family business He has called, equipped and empowered us to take an active role in, as born-again, Spirit-filled believers.

AUTHORITY

A good understanding of authority is essential if we are to exercise an effective healing ministry and this is dealt with in more detail in Chapter 6. For now, let us just consider two verses in Luke's Gospel that highlight authority, both in the ministry of Jesus Himself and in the ministry to which He called the original 12 disciples, the 70 whom He sent out on mission – and each one of us:

> All the people were amazed and said to each other, 'What words these are! With **authority** and power he gives orders to impure spirits and they come out!'
>
> (Luke 4:36)

> When Jesus had called the Twelve together, he gave them power and **authority** to drive out all demons and to cure diseases, and he sent them out to proclaim the kingdom of God and to heal those who were ill.
>
> (Luke 9:1–2)

There is another point I would like to make here, in the context of authority. Nowhere in the Gospels will we find Jesus offering up a *prayer* for the sick. Neither will you find an instance of Him calling believers to pray for the sick. Reading Acts, you will find no examples of the apostles and others praying for the sick. In Matthew 10 Jesus says we are to *heal* the sick. We do that by making commands and declarations with authority, just as He did. I can find only one instance of praying for the sick in the Bible and that is in James 5, in the context of calling for the elders to pray.

Taking such authority can be one of the more difficult practices for us to adopt, along with ministering with our *eyes open*, when we take our first steps into healing ministry. If you have not 'prayed' in that manner before, and it is not a common practice in the church tradition you are part of, it is especially difficult. But it is not impossible. Once we understand that we are exercising the authority which Jesus has delegated to us, not our own, it becomes increasingly easier to do, especially alongside the positive 'results' it will bring to encourage us.

EXAMPLE

Jesus set us an example to follow in the three years or so that He ministered on earth as the **Son of Man**. You will recall that this is the term He used most often when speaking of Himself. It is very significant, because we need to understand that Jesus ministered as a *man*, not as God, thereby setting an example we could follow. If He had ministered only as God, what He did would still be highly impressive, but we would have no hope of emulating Him.

> God anointed Jesus of Nazareth with the Holy Spirit and power, and … he went around doing good and **healing** all who were under the power of the devil, because God was with him.
>
> (Acts 10:38)

I believe that verse is a deliberate illustration of the ministry of Jesus as a man. Yes, He was, is and always will be the Son of God, but for 30-something years He laid aside His majesty, His deity, and 'tabernacled' (lived) among us. It was only as the perfect, sinless *man* that He could be the adequate sacrifice for sin – and for sickness. He was a man in whom, on whom and through whom Holy Spirit was given without measure. As the Son of Man, He could authoritatively and prophetically promise that we would be able to do the works that He did on earth:

Very truly I tell you, whoever believes in me will do the works I have been doing, and they will do even greater things than these, because I am going to the Father.

(John 14:12)

He even talks about 'greater' works. Now we can speculate until the cows come home as to what these greater works might be. Some have suggested, as an example, that there is nothing in scripture to indicate that He *eradicated* a disease from the earth, but He has since gifted medical science with the ability to do that! We don't need to be injected against smallpox any more, for instance. No doubt readers who are more knowledgeable than I about medicine can provide many more examples.

There are several diseases, cancer for example, that are not specifically mentioned in the Bible but are both known and healed today, so it may even be that Jesus had this in mind when He spoke those words. What we do know is that the Greek word translated 'greater' generally refers to *quantity*, not quality.

Whatever the true answer may be, my suggestion is that we seek to discover what the greater things are by doing all we can to minister healing, persistently pressing in for breakthroughs in areas where we have not yet encountered 'success'. Often, we reach breakthrough through a process rather than by means of an immediate experience, not something any of us accept very easily in this 'instant' age.

CHALLENGE

Cathy and I were encouraged to explore the healing ministry by the following verse and I will never tire of using it as an illustration that encapsulates what healing ministry is about:

> As you go, proclaim this message: 'The kingdom of heaven has come near.' Heal those who are ill, raise the dead, cleanse those who have leprosy, drive out demons. **Freely you have received; freely give**.
>
> (Matthew 10:7–8)

Who says that we are qualified to do this? Jesus, the One who qualified us, by and through His amazing grace alone! Yes, we can all do it. Indeed, we are all meant to do it. If we want to play our part in seeing Heaven's Health Manifesto implemented on planet earth, we should begin taking an active part in the healing ministry and be determined to carry on – no matter what.

Sadly, not every church family has embraced this philosophy of healing as a part of normal, everyday Christian life. That can be a real challenge for those of us who are members of such a church. Heavenly wisdom is needed to make the right decision about whether to stay or to move on.

David Webster (one of the leaders at Eastgate) has said that, 'We accept the culture/beliefs of the church that we are born again into.' One would hardly expect anything else, because that is where the foundations of our faith are built. But we should have the freedom to ask questions and to explore options, especially if the prevalent culture is challenged by a new (to us) revelation that is biblically based.

If you find yourself in this difficult situation, my advice is to lay it before God in prayer, ideally supported by Christians friends, and follow your heart.

NOTES

[1] I do not like the NIV translation here ('demon-possessed'). Many commentators consider the word 'demonised' to be a much more accurate reflection

of the Greek original. 'Possession' implies a much more serious level of demonic affliction than most instances will involve. 'Oppression' is a much more appropriate term for the vast majority of cases that you and I are likely to encounter.

Chapter 6

AUTHORITY

All authority in heaven and on earth has been given to me.
Therefore [you] go and ...

(Matthew 28:18–19)

M Y EARLIEST EXPERIENCES, AS AN OBSERVER, of demons being expelled were usually marked by lots of noise (on both sides) and what often appeared to be a long and exhausting power battle. It seemed to achieve the desired result, most of the time, but not without a huge amount of effort being expended.

I think this is because these encounters had more to do with **power** than **authority**. The victory of Jesus at the cross did not simply rob the enemy of his ultimate power; more significantly, it took back the authority he stole from human beings, by deception, back in Genesis at the time of the Fall.

On the occasions that Cathy and I have ministered deliverance we have focused upon removing the ground, the foundation, upon which the demon stood in a person's life; then taking authority over it, in the name of Jesus, and telling it to go. On each occasion, the expulsion has been quick and has rarely involved more than a cough or a sneeze, if any manifestation at all. I am firmly convinced that this is because we have learned to approach such confrontations as authority, rather than power, encounters.

Now, in fairness, we have yet to minister to someone who has been deeply involved in the occult or has had connection with major issues, like Satanism, so I am not saying there might *never* be any 'fireworks', but rather that it need not be so every time – if we focus correctly.

A helpful illustration of the difference between power and authority, especially if you are of a certain age and can remember seeing this, is the policeman on point duty, directing traffic. The job is invariably done by traffic lights now, of course, unless they have broken down! The traffic policeman could stop a huge lorry or bus by simply raising a hand. He did not do it in his own strength (power) as if he could physically halt the vehicle, but by his authority, made plain to all by the uniform he wore to represent his position in the community.

So, let us take a brief biblical overview of the subject of authority, beginning back in the book of Genesis and an encounter between Adam, Eve and a certain slippery serpent.

Although Adam and Eve committed no sin until after they were deceived, I hesitate to say that they were created perfect, sinless in the sense of being incapable of sin. Rightly or wrongly, I prefer to use the term 'innocent'. The fact that they committed no sin until they succumbed to temptation implies (to me) that they must have been vulnerable to falling at any time by making a wrong choice.

Falling into sin was not inevitable, but neither was it impossible, because they had been given free will.

They were the pinnacle of God's creation, the 'very good' part, and they were given authority. This was delegated to them, by God, so that they could exercise that authority over the rest of creation:

> Then God said, 'Let us make mankind in our image, in our likeness, so that they may rule over the fish in the sea and the birds in the sky, over the livestock and all the wild animals, and over all the creatures that move along the ground.
>
> (Genesis 1:26)

Indeed, Adam was even given the task of naming the animals, reflecting an emerging culture where names carried far more significance than they do now – in Western cultures, at least. I believe that the names Adam chose influenced both the nature and the character of each creature, serving as more than just a means of identification, like 'Spot', 'Tiddles' or 'Fido'.

But the devil entered the Garden, in the form of a serpent, and proceeded to deceive the couple. In the process, he usurped their God-given authority, taking it for himself. Sin entered the world, resulting in mankind's separation from God. Even then God had a plan of redemption prepared to deal with this eventuality, although it would not fully come into play until many years later, of course.

Eventually, beginning with Abraham, God set apart the nation of Israel for a special relationship with Him, through whom He could enjoy a level of communication with mankind. Albeit that the Israelites invariably conspired to make that relationship as difficult as possible to maintain without Him exercising amazing grace.

As we know, approximately two thousand years ago, all the prophecies about a Messiah, a Deliverer, a Saviour, were fulfilled with the incarnation of the Son of God in the form of Jesus of Nazareth, the Son of Man. When He encountered the devil in the wilderness, the Bible makes clear that the devil still had the authority he had stolen from Adam and Eve centuries before:

> And he said to him, '**I** will give you all their authority and splendour; it has been given to me, and **I** can give it to anyone **I** want to. So if you worship me, it will all be yours.
>
> (Luke 4:6)

The significance of this part of the encounter is that Jesus made no attempt to dispute the claim the devil made regarding his position of authority. He accepted it as a fact, although Jesus knew that it would not be long before His mission would be accomplished, and the status quo restored. This result is made clear in the Great Commission at the end of Matthew's Gospel:

> Then Jesus came to them and said, '**All** authority in heaven and on earth has been given to me. Therefore [you] go and ...
>
> (Matthew 28:18–19)

Sorry to labour the point about the word 'all', but it does mean exactly what it says. In this context, it means that the devil no longer has any authority, although he is more than capable of deceiving mankind into believing he has. We must remember, Christians especially, that the devil only has authority over us to the extent that we come into *agreement* with him and his lies.

So, it is vitally important for us to understand the present situation if we are to minister effectively, whether in healing the sick or in other areas. When Jesus won back all authority from the devil it was accomplished for our benefit, not for His. He never lost His authority as the Son of God. Heaven was not affected by the Fall. God never ceased to be Almighty God. There is just no contest in any conflict between God and the devil, a created being.

When He came to bring Heaven to earth, Jesus did so with the authority invested in Him, as the Son of Man, by the Father and in the power of Holy Spirit. It was this authority that He began to delegate to His followers even before His victory on the cross, His resurrection, His ascension and the coming of Holy Spirit at Pentecost. We see the evidence of this when He commissioned both the Twelve and the Seventy:

> When Jesus had called the Twelve together, he gave them power and **authority** to drive out all demons and to cure diseases, and he sent them out to proclaim the kingdom of God and to heal those who were ill.
>
> (Luke 9:1–2)

> I have given you **authority** to trample on snakes and scorpions1 and to overcome all the power of the enemy …
>
> (Luke 10:19)

Then, as we read again the Great Commission in Matthew 28, we find that this applies not only to the disciples who were present at the time but also to all those believers to whom they would pass on all the commands and teachings of Jesus. We find it also, of course, in the verses at the end of Mark 16, which I quote several times in this writing.

Furthermore, we see evidence of the authority vested in us, and delegated to us, in the basic gospel message of reconciliation to God. You see, the Greek word *exousia*, translated as 'right' in the NIV version of the verse below, may also be translated as 'power' or 'authority'. The use of either 'right' or 'authority' could be made here without losing the truth of what is being conveyed by John. We are born again into authority by Jesus' authority.

> Yet to all who received him, to those who believed in his name, he gave the right to become children of God ...

(John 1:12, NIV 1984)

Miracles are a *demonstration of authority*, as well as of the Kingdom (the King's dominion) being released on earth (see John 10:37–38, for example). As we read through the Gospels we come across a great number of healings and deliverances, which Jesus ministered to those who followed Him, as well as the accounts of what both the Twelve and the Seventy experienced.

Jesus was the model, the template, for the born-again, Spirit-filled Christian of today. The evidence for this is found throughout the book of Acts where we find many examples of the apostles, and others, doing what Jesus had done, exercising the authority He had delegated to them (and to us). We come across many instances of this, also, down through two thousand years of church history. During some periods, such instances have been rare, but they have never ceased completely. God has never left Himself without a witness.

The authority that has been delegated to us is not something to be used to 'control' others. We do not have authority 'over' someone. It is given to us in the context of **service**. Authority and submission (biblical submission is mutual submission) do indeed go together, but the correct outworking of this requires godly wisdom.

The important thing to bear in mind is that the authority we are given should increase freedom, not restrict it. Nevertheless, our freedom must always be tempered by responsibility and exercised in a godly way. (Note: Freedom without Responsibility = Anarchy.)

God does not dictate how we should live, even though He always knows best, but rather we make our own choices. He has absolute authority, but He gives us freedom of choice; He does not *control* us. So, it is up to us to use both freedom and authority in a responsible way, never to control others. There can be no freedom without choice. Adam and Eve were the first to use their God-given freedom to make a wrong choice.

We are to exercise authority, as directed, without ever being controlling or 'lording' it over people. As already stated, this is to be done through serving and, clearly, freedom with responsibility is intended to operate in the same context. The wrong use of authority produces control, legalism and religion rather than freedom and life. This is in complete contrast to the purpose of Jesus (see John 10:10, for example).

So, when we have the freedom to exercise the authority delegated to us we need safeguards, both in the church and in everyday life. But safeguards, or boundaries if you like, are not rules! Let me state it again: rules lead us into legalism and religion. The godly exercise of authority brings freedom and life.

When miracles are performed, when the sick are healed, this is a basic demonstration of Kingdom authority. Jesus is getting what He paid the full price for. If it were not for the devil and the Fall, there would be no sickness or death.[2] Jesus has won back all authority once and forever, positionally.

But, *experientially*, a gradual process in our lives is the norm. We see the evidence bit by bit because, although Jesus paid the price once and forever, we usually enter into the reality of His victory gradually, as part of our daily experience of life. A succession of little victories, within the context of a war already won, tends to mark our progression into greater Christian maturity.

We still sin and get sick from time to time, don't we? But: 'The reason the Son of God appeared was to destroy the devil's work' (1 John 3:8).

This has been accomplished once and forever, which is why we can be sure that we have been delegated authority over sickness, even over death. But the presence of sickness and death was not removed from the world in one fell swoop at Calvary. We enter into that victory experience when we exercise faith and authority in His name to destroy the residues of the devil's work as and when we come across them.

Now, the authority we have had delegated to us is ours by **grace**. It is to be exercised under the guidance and direction of Holy Spirit. If we resort to certain words, phrases or formulae, bypassing our dependence upon Him, we step into the realm of **works**, not grace.

Let me include a cautionary word here, please. We need to be careful when we read about the encounter between Jesus and the centurion (see Matthew 8:5–13) and the references to authority here. The centurion recognised that Jesus had authority over sickness. But when he told Jesus that He had only to 'say the word' to heal his servant, the centurion was exercising **faith**. So, this passage is not about being 'under' authority, like his soldiers, but about faith in the ability of Jesus to exercise His Kingdom authority over sickness to heal the servant.

Although John 17:2 informs us that Jesus has authority over all people, it goes on to clarify that this is to give Life, not to take control. There are no verses in our Bibles which say that Jesus has authority *over* an individual. This would be to deny the freedom we are given to take authority over our own lives and to make our own choices (and to bear responsibility for those choices).

In general terms, authority must fit into the framework of freedom. Within the context of healing ministry, we exercise authority over sickness to bring freedom (from sickness) to the person we minister to. We do not exercise authority over that person. They are free to either submit to or reject our offer to help them into breakthrough. This freedom of choice must always be respected.

You will notice how this view contrasts with a hierarchical society concept, one which many churches embrace. Submission, in the Bible, is always linked with authority but, in a hierarchical setting, submission means that a person is 'under' someone who is in authority 'over' them, and this easily leads to **control**.

So, Jesus has authority over death, sickness and demons. *We* don't – in and of ourselves. We utilise His authority, which has been delegated to us. By faith, we exercise His authority over sickness to heal the sick. By faith, we exercise His authority over demons to expel them. By faith, we exercise His authority over death to raise the dead.

But, before we do any of that, we listen for the prompting, guiding and leading of Holy Spirit (just as Jesus did during His ministry on earth as the Son of Man) and we step out in faith and in obedience to Him. We do this knowing who and whose we are, not out of effort but from a position of surrender to Him that has been developed through growing intimacy.

In every area where we have been enabled to gain experience, we will increase in authority. Skills increase with experience, but authority does not. Full authority was delegated to us when we were born again, so we simply explore more of the outworking of that grace as we grow in ministry.

To summarise, then, we have been delegated the authority that Jesus won back from the devil on our behalf and we use it to do the works of Jesus, who came to destroy the works of the devil and has commissioned us to do the same. And, to paraphrase the many gambling advertisements, use your authority *responsibly* – to the glory of God.

NOTES

[1] Trampling on 'snakes and scorpions' may be taken literally but my own thinking agrees with those who interpret this as referring to the demonic realm.

[2] I do not mean that all sickness and death is demonic in origin, in the sense that it is always caused by a demon, or demons attacking or oppressing a person. That is possible but it is not inevitable. I certainly believe that the devil is at the root of all sickness and death in the world, but his minions are not necessarily directly active in every individual manifestation of sickness and death.

We can deal appropriately with demons if we find them, but we do not have to minister with the primary purpose of seeking them out. This can become an unfortunate obsession for some, which should be avoided. Never make the demonic the focus of your ministry or you can find yourself playing into the demons' hands. They are attention-seekers (and liars) and you could become a victim of deception yourself if you make the mistake of unnecessarily engaging in dialogue with them.

Chapter 7

THE FULL GOSPEL

Therefore go and make disciples of all nations, baptising them in the name of the Father and of the Son and of the Holy Spirit, and teaching them to obey everything I have commanded you.

(Matthew 28:19–20)

IT IS MORE THAN 45 YEARS NOW SINCE I became a Christian; since I knew that God had forgiven my sins through the death of His Son, and I was born again through the work of Holy Spirit and experienced the joy of a restored relationship with Father God. A year later I was baptised in Holy Spirit and spoke in tongues for the first time.

This is evidence of a wonderful, marvellous work of grace that is as true today as it was when it all began for me back in May 1971. But I do not believe that it encompasses the full gospel! To understand what is meant by that expression, it helps to understand a little Greek.

The Greek word *sozo* is usually understood to mean 'salvation' and that is often interpreted, by well-meaning theologians and speakers, solely as the 'forgiveness of sins'. In fact, there are three strands to the full meaning of this Greek word, not one. *Sozo* encompasses **forgiveness**, **healing** and **deliverance**, and that combination is what I deem to be the full gospel.[1] The Greek translation into our English Bibles demonstrates this diversity:

> If you declare with your mouth, 'Jesus is Lord,' and believe in your heart that God raised him from the dead, you will be **saved** [*sozo*].

> (Romans 10:9)

> Jesus turned and saw her. 'Take heart, daughter,' he said, 'your faith has healed you.' And the woman was **healed** [*sozo*] at that moment.

> (Matthew 9:22)

> Those who had seen it told the people how the [demonised] man had been [**delivered**] [*sozo*].

> (Luke 8:36)

When I tackle this subject in a workshop, I like to use an illustration of the three-fold meaning of *sozo* alongside the Three 'I's dealt with in Chapter 4 of this book: Identity + Intimacy = Impact. Seeing these two concepts side by side shows us what it takes to understand, proclaim and demonstrate the full gospel. This is what each one of us is called to do as a natural part of the fundamentally normal, everyday Christian life.

It is incumbent upon every preacher of the gospel, in my opinion, to include all three elements in his or her proclamation of

Sozo	*I*
Saved/Forgiven	Identity
Healed	Intimacy
Delivered	Impact

the Kingdom message, but the focus of this book is upon healing, of course.

In Acts 17 we read of the time Paul spent in Athens, and a lot of space is given over to the nub of the message he preached there. Indeed, I am given to understand that many Bible colleges use this message as *the* model sermon. We are told that a few men believed (not a typical 'result' for Paul's preaching!) and then the scene shifts immediately to Corinth. So, what Paul writes in his first letter to the Corinthians is quite revealing, especially in the opening verses of chapter 2.

Here, under the inspiration of Holy Spirit, Paul reminds his readers that he did not come to them with eloquent words, aiming to impress them with his wisdom. This is what would have been expected of him in Athens and, there, to some extent, he seems to have done just that. His Athenian listeners in that city were all interested in hearing the latest thing, in debating the latest philosophical fads of the day. They were easily drawn to human wisdom and eloquence rather than matters of spiritual substance and, consequently, the interest of most of them was only fleeting.

It is my belief that Paul felt that his approach in Athens was possibly not the best one, even for the Greek culture of his day, so he resolved to change it at his next port of call, Corinth. His Corinthian hearers may not have had the intellectual sophistication of the Athenians, but I don't think it was this fact alone that prompted Paul to change his approach.

Rather, in my opinion, it was his personal disappointment with the results of his ministry in Athens, and the regrettable way he went about it, that brought the marked change of emphasis.

> When I came to you, I did not come with eloquence or human wisdom as I proclaimed to you the testimony about God. For I resolved to know nothing while I was with you except Jesus Christ and him crucified. I came to you in weakness with great fear and trembling. My message and my preaching were not with wise and persuasive **words**, but with a demonstration of the Spirit's **power**, so that your faith might not rest on human wisdom, but on God's power.
>
> (1 Corinthians 2:1–5)

We know, with the benefit of biblical revelation, that the church in Corinth was not without its problems but, nevertheless, it seems very clear to me that Paul's evangelistic efforts in Corinth bore considerably more fruit than did his preaching in Athens. There is no doubt, in my mind, that this is because of the demonstration of the power of Holy Spirit.

Some will argue that this refers to the anointing upon the words spoken by Paul, but I am more inclined to see this as evidence of his apostleship. 'I persevered in demonstrating among you the marks of a true apostle, including **signs**, **wonders** and **miracles**,' he writes in 2 Corinthians 12:12. This is also made clear in 1 Corinthians 4:20, albeit in a slightly different context: 'For the kingdom of God is not a matter of talk but of power.'

We do not see anywhere in the account of his visit to Athens that 'the marks of a true apostle' were evident. But in Corinth, I believe, they were, and they made all the difference to the response from his first hearers there.

It is not enough, I am suggesting, for an evangelist or evangelistic preacher to proclaim what he or she believes in words alone,
no matter how eloquent and anointed those words may be. There
needs to be a demonstration of what is believed. These are the signs
of the full gospel being proclaimed, the gospel of the Kingdom, of
Heaven invading earth.

We see this demonstrated in the ministry of the Son of Man.
The ministry of Jesus' earliest disciples continued in the same vein.
They have passed on the baton, down through the ages, to pres-
ent-day believers like you and me.

You may remember that, when John the Baptist was impris-
oned, he began to have doubts about Jesus as the authentic Messiah
and sent his disciples to gain assurance for him. What happened
is recorded in Matthew 11:2–6:

> When John, who was in prison, heard about the deeds of the
> Messiah, he sent his disciples to ask him, 'Are you the one
> who is to come, or should we expect someone else?' Jesus
> replied, 'Go back and report to John what you hear and
> see: the blind receive sight, the lame walk, those who have
> leprosy are cleansed, the deaf hear, the dead are raised, and
> the good news is proclaimed to the poor. Blessed is anyone
> who does not stumble on account of me.'

Jesus does not refer the disciples of John to the words He spoke,
even though the crowds found His teaching remarkable, but to
the things He did. His miraculous deeds were hard evidence of
both His Messiahship and that the Kingdom of Heaven was at
hand.

He does indeed mention that the good news (**forgiveness**?)
was proclaimed to the poor, but greater emphasis is given here to
works of **healing**, which may well have included **deliverance** as
part of the process. We know that it did on many occasions during

His ministry. So, here we find that Jesus is demonstrating the full gospel Himself, not only to bless the people but also by way of example to all those who would follow Him.

When we read Matthew 10:7–8 and Luke 10:1 and 9 we see that Jesus gave both the Twelve and the Seventy essentially the same assignment. They were to preach a message, yes, but they were also given authority to heal the sick and cast out demons. That is the full gospel once again. And, of course, this was happening before Jesus was crucified, resurrected and ascended and before Holy Spirit had been poured out, as prophesied in Joel 2.

Going on to Matthew 28:18–20, to what has now become known as the Great Commission (perhaps better expressed as Co-Mission), we find Jesus giving His disciples the command to '*Go!*', to make more disciples and teach them to say and do all that Jesus had taught them to say and do. The words of the full gospel message will be confirmed by the demonstration of the full gospel (see Mark 16:20 for confirmation of this). Signs following the proclamation of the Word are both 'the marks of an apostle' and the marks of a believer such as you and me.

After the ascension of Jesus and the birth of the church on the Day of Pentecost, we find that the Twelve, now known as the apostles, were obedient to the mission Jesus entrusted to them. Acts 5:12–16 is just one scriptural confirmation that they did preach and demonstrate the full gospel:

> The apostles performed many **signs** and **wonders** among the people. And all the believers used to meet together in Solomon's Colonnade. No one else dared join them, even though they were highly regarded by the people. Nevertheless, more and more men and women believed in the Lord and were added to their number. As a result, people brought those who were ill into the streets and laid them

on beds and mats so that at least Peter's shadow might fall on some of them as he passed by. Crowds gathered also from the towns around Jerusalem, bringing those who were ill and those tormented by impure spirits, and all of them were **healed**.

What we need to realise here, in case we are still in doubt about our own calling as believers, is that the demonstration of the full gospel was not to be confined to Jesus and the Twelve. We find evidence of this as we read on in Acts about Stephen, Philip and Paul, for example. I realise that Paul describes himself as an apostle, and I certainly do not dispute his right to do so, but he was not one of the 12 disciples who received the initial calling.

Now **Stephen**, a man full of God's grace and power, performed great wonders and signs among the people.

(Acts 6:8)

Stephen was one of the seven deacons appointed by the Twelve to help resolve a dispute over the distribution of food to the widows fed by the church.

Philip went down to a city in Samaria and proclaimed the Messiah there. When the crowds heard Philip, and saw the signs he performed, they all paid close attention to what he said. For with shrieks, impure spirits came out of many, and many who were paralysed or lame were healed. So, there was great joy in that city … Simon [a man who had practised sorcery] himself believed and was baptised. And he followed Philip everywhere, astonished by the great signs and miracles he saw.

(Acts 8:5–8, 13)

Philip was also one of the seven deacons, later to be described as an evangelist and the father of four unmarried daughters who prophesied (Acts 21:8–9). He should not be confused with the Philip who was one of the original 12 disciples (John 1:44) and came from Bethsaida.

I have already mentioned **Paul**, of course, but there are a couple of other scriptures I would like to add to emphasise the point I am making in this chapter about what the full gospel is.

> God did extraordinary miracles through Paul, so that even handkerchiefs and aprons that had touched him were taken to those who were ill, and their illnesses were cured and the evil spirits left them.
>
> (Acts 19:11–12)

> I will not venture to speak of anything except what Christ has accomplished through me in leading the Gentiles to obey God by what I have said **and** done – by the power of signs and wonders, through the power of the Spirit of God. So from Jerusalem all the way round to Illyricum, I have **fully** proclaimed the gospel of Christ.
>
> (Romans 15:18–19)

Finally, within the scriptures, we come to *all* believers, the category in which you and I are included. If we are believers, we cannot claim that this call of God to recognise and practise the healing ministry does not apply to us as much as to those mentioned above. I am not necessarily talking about a 'specialist' healing ministry, but a gift to be exercised with faith by any one of us, as and when God provides the opportunity.

I want to illustrate this from Mark's Gospel as well as from a random selection of people from church history, right down to the present day and you and me. It is so important that we do not find an excuse to exclude ourselves from what God has provided, by grace alone, for our inheritance *now* as His children.

> And these signs will accompany [**all**] those who believe: In my name they will drive out demons … they will place their hands on sick people, and they will get well.' … Then the disciples went out and preached everywhere, and the Lord worked with them and confirmed his word by the signs that accompanied it.
>
> (Mark 16:17a, 18b, 20, NIV 1984)

EARLY CHURCH FATHERS

There are many recorded testimonies of healing and deliverance in the writings of people like Clement, Irenaeus, Tertullian and Origen, although I am limiting myself to just one quote here. However, I would encourage you to make your own study to verify these assertions.

> Healing is a natural activity of Christians as they express the creative power of God given them as members of Christ.
>
> (Irenaeus)

GEORGE FOX

This gentleman is probably best known as the founder of the Quakers. He swam against the strong tide of the church in his day and paid a considerable price for his faith as he took a firm stand for the truth of the Word of God, both by proclamation and demonstration. Today we can so easily take for granted the Kingdom benefits we have received because of the price paid for them in the past by Fox,

Wesley, Whitfield and many more. We should not squander the privileges granted to us by the sacrifices they made.

MARIAH WOODWORTH-ETTER

This amazing lady was a healing evangelist in an age where it simply was not the 'done' thing for a woman to preach or minister in the church. Her remarkable meetings, very often conducted in the face of great and violent opposition, were marked by impressive healings and deliverances. They became infamous for the large numbers of people 'slain in the Spirit' when Holy Spirit moved in power in the ministry tents with which she toured the USA in the late nineteenth and early twentieth centuries.

Here is another who paid the price for breakthrough. Women in the church today are experiencing, almost universally, the freedoms that ladies like Mother Etter won for them with their pioneering spirit and determination to follow the will of God, whatever the cost.

JOHN G. LAKE

Lake was an extremely successful businessman who gave up wealth and prestige to preach the gospel and heal the sick. He was greatly used by God in revival in South Africa in the early 1900s, after travelling from the USA without the resources to complete even the outward trip. There was no support from any missionary organisation and nowhere to live with his wife and six children on arrival. God provided everything they needed, including a family home, and released such a powerful anointing that countless numbers were saved, healed and delivered under his ministry.

He returned from South Africa a widower, married again, and pioneered the Healing Rooms ministry in Spokane, Washington, around the time of the First World War. God so used him and his team of helpers that, within a few years, Spokane was declared by the US government to be the healthiest city in the United States! Even in those days, people were travelling from around the world to visit the Healing Rooms, which he also opened later in Portland, Oregon.

Sadly, after his death in 1935, the ministry died until, some 60 years later, God called Cal and Michelle Pierce to leave Bethel Church in Redding, California, and travel up to Spokane to 're-dig the wells' of Lake's Healing Rooms. The IAHR (International Association of Healing Rooms) ministry has since spread across the USA and into Europe.

Cathy and I have had the privilege of visiting a typical Healing Rooms in the UK to observe how they operate. We were also delighted to be asked to participate in ministry there and saw God move to heal and restore several people in just one evening, thanks to the service of a dedicated team.

AIMEE SEMPLE-MCPHERSON

This lady became the founder of the Foursquare Gospel churches, and her flamboyant ministry in the Angelus Temple that she built in Los Angeles even touched the hearts of Hollywood stars. Healing miracles marked her ministry, even from its early, impoverished days. She never took 'No' for an answer when she believed God was calling her to do something for Him and she was willing to pay the price for her obedience. Controversy was rarely a stranger to her life but there is no doubt that she was a remarkable woman of God, another who paved the way for women to step out of the shadows of husbands and fathers to serve the Lord in their own callings.

We have English friends in Red Bluff, California, who were called to plant a church in that city after two years at the Bethel

School of Supernatural Ministry. They began their meetings in their own home and, after growing out of that and several other locations, their current base is a Foursquare church originally commissioned by Sister Aimee back in 1928.

We have another friend who, on a recent trip to Burma (Myanmar) to minister to a group of Foursquare churches there, reported stories of healings, signs and wonders by the power of God in various locations. What is so encouraging, for us, is that *Alec* is the husband of the lady whose healing at Detling in 2009 helped to lead him to respond to the challenge to take this aspect of ministry to Burma and Thailand on his future visits abroad!

SMITH WIGGLESWORTH

There cannot be many Christians in the world who have not heard of this remarkable man and his ministry, which really did not fully take off until after the death of his wife when they were both in their fifties. There are at least 15 verified cases of people being raised from the dead through this man of amazing faith and obedience whose byword was 'Only believe!' His long and active life in ministry ended when he was in his late eighties and, if ever anyone lived a life of preaching and demonstrating the full gospel, it was this bluff, gruff ex-plumber from Bradford.

Sadly, the only legacy of his ministry, apart from many books, seems to be a museum in Bradford. It is such a shame that we so rarely see a ministry being continued by others following the death of the original pioneer. Now that we are in an era where ministries dependent upon one man or woman (humanly speaking) are less prevalent than before, maybe we will begin to see greater longevity in respect of ministries, more likened to a movement involving many participants. I certainly hope and pray that will be the case.

KATHRYN KUHLMAN

Miss Kuhlman probably had one of the better-known healing ministries of the twentieth century. It was marked by her total devotion to Holy Spirit, His guidance and direction, especially after the blip caused by her brief and seemingly unwise marriage. She ministered mainly through the word of knowledge, much as Todd Bentley did in the Lakeland meetings through which I was healed in 2008. People were healed where they sat; often she would call out what she sensed Holy Spirit to be doing and in what part of the auditorium He was moving in power. There would also be many people in wheelchairs lined up at the front in her meetings. She rejoiced over those who were healed and wept over those who were not. Her influence was felt by and inspired many others, including the Happy Hunters and Benny Hinn.

GEORGE JEFFRIES

Along with his brother and others, George Jeffries was a founder of the Elim movement and had a remarkable healing ministry. At one time, he had annual meetings in the Royal Albert Hall that filled the auditorium to capacity and there were many great healing testimonies arising out of these meetings. In later life, a very young Reinhardt Bonnke sought him out in London on his way home from Bible College in the UK. Whatever happened to him?

BILL JOHNSON[2]

It amazes me that I can still come across people who have not heard of this man, let alone been influenced by the teaching and culture he has helped to create, under God, through being the senior pastor

of Bethel Church in Redding, California. I was introduced to him
through his early books, very soon after the ME healing, and I
continue to read anything I can that is produced by this remarkable
preacher, teacher and example.

He has gathered many gifted people around him at Bethel,
and elsewhere, and the unique ministries of each one of them
have blessed me. The influence of the 'Bethel Culture' continues
to expand around the world and, while I understand that there
is no perfect church this side of Heaven, these believers must
come close.

Students from many countries attend BSSM (the Bethel School
of Supernatural Ministry). God has really blessed me through people
like Danny Silk, Kris Vallotton, Joaquin Evans, Dawna da Silva
and Chuck Parry, to name but a few. First-year students at ESSL
are inspired by at least one teaching DVD each week from such
men and women of faith.

Johnson's breakthrough book was *When Heaven Invades Earth*
– a title that probably sums up very well what the whole Bethel
ministry stands for. Later books, co-written with the likes of Randy
Clark, such as *Healing: Unplugged*, could not come more highly
recommended by this avid reader of them. Whenever I feel I am
in danger of being undermined by discouragement or disappointment, I go and get a Bill Johnson book off the shelf and head
for the bathroom and a long, hot soak in the presence of God
while I feed and renew my mind with Holy Spirit inspired
wisdom.

There are countless people alive and healthy today who
would have been just the opposite if God had not caused them to
encounter somebody either from or influenced by Bethel. What
better legacy could a ministry have than that? They encourage the
younger generation to build their floor upon the ceiling of the older
generation. In other words, they pass on a legacy.

JAMES MALONEY

A few years back, just after we had heard that James Maloney was coming to speak at North Kent Community Church (now Eastgate), I was at a conference they ran with Bill Johnson as the main speaker. During one of his discourses Bill referred to the imminent visit of this man – at that time unknown (to me) – describing him as 'the person who carries the greatest anointing for miracles I have come across to date'. Since then I have heard James Maloney speak at meetings on a couple of occasions and on TV. I can now testify that he not only carries an amazing anointing for healing and miracles but also the most extraordinary prophetic gifting.

I recommend his book *The Dancing Hand of God* as a brilliant introduction to his exciting life story and an account of some of the marvellous things God has done both in and through him. The healing of a toddler with dwarfism is a remarkable story on several levels and worth the price of the book on its own! I still often tell myself his story of the Indian man who had a hand and a shoulder, but no arm in between, until a very reluctant young female team-member prayed for him. She did so with her eyes firmly shut and did not see the hand coming towards her head as it shot out on the end of a brand-new arm. This just goes to show that the healing ministry literally packs quite a punch!

PAUL BENNISON

Paul is a friend of ours with whom we have had the privilege of ministering on several occasions. He has been travelling all over the world for more than 30 years and has seen many people saved, healed and delivered. Never heard of him? He likes it that way. He doesn't seek the big platforms or prestigious events. You are more likely to find him in the back streets and the slums when he travels abroad. He has seen God do amazing things, particularly in Cali, Colombia, including ministering healing to everyone in the children's ward of a local hospital on one memorable afternoon!

One lady in that city (for whom he has raised funds to expand her ministry) has opened her home to elderly people who have been abandoned on the streets by their families. She feeds, clothes and cares for them, doing everything by faith, as she has no government support. She has had terminal cancer at least three times and, on each occasion, Paul has ministered to her on his next visit after the latest diagnosis, and she has been completely healed! In addition, he has been used by God in Colombia to raise both a young boy and an elderly lady from the dead!

As I write this, Cathy and I are less than one month away from joining Paul, and other team members, on a trip to Cali. We are very much looking forward to hearing, seeing and experiencing Holy Spirit at work in what Paul describes as an 'open heaven' location.

He has chosen not to publish a book, which is sad (I think) because his stories of the goodness of God are such an encouragement, both to us and to every believer who wants to see more of the Kingdom manifested in his or her own life. He has paid, and continues to pay, quite a price for the fruit of his ministry but he remains true to his calling and so God just increases the anointing on his life.

EASTGATE

Pete Carter is a qualified doctor as well as being one of the 'directors' of Eastgate, our home church. He has a vision for the healing ministry of the church being aligned with the National Health Service in the UK and is actively pursuing such a link between local medical professionals and the Healing Centre at Eastgate. This is currently open on the first and third Saturday mornings of each month and Cathy and I are privileged to serve on the team in that heavenly environment.

Pete's vision is for the NHS to be able to refer patients to the Healing Centre, especially if they are deemed to be beyond conventional medical help. 'Heaven in Healthcare' is just one of the initiatives coming out of that vision, starting with an annual conference and with the obvious potential to expand on both a national and international level.

Among the many varied and medically verified healing testimonies coming out of the Healing Centre, there are a growing number from people who have made a full recovery from terminal cancer.

Pete has also written a book, *Unwrapping Lazarus*, which opens with stories of him being used by God in Mexico to bring healing to a quadriplegic teenager and a dead baby. These two stories alone contain several valuable lessons for all who aspire to answer the call of God to heal the sick. Much excellent teaching can be found throughout the book.

The Eastgate School of Supernatural Life encourages and trains people to operate under the guidance and power of Holy Spirit. Students go out every week into nearby Gravesend to minister on the streets. In addition, they go on at least two four-day mission trips per year, either within the UK or abroad, to minister God's love to people both within and outside the church walls.

One of the main reasons why I signed up for the day school was because, although more than comfortable speaking to a crowd in church, a one-to-one encounter with a complete stranger was very daunting for me. God met and encouraged me in an amazing way before and during my first two ESSL Treasure Hunts and I have not looked back since!

DENNIS AND CATHY ACOTT

It is so encouraging to find that God is moving away from the big-name platform ministries of the past into a new season where ordinary people doing extraordinary things all over the world are re-presenting Him and the full gospel. These are exciting times and we can share in them, as workers sent into the harvest field, if we will only rise to the challenge. We do not have to travel the world to find needy people. They are already on our doorsteps, in our cities, towns and villages; anywhere we may go, every day of our lives. Our own Eagles 4031 ministry is designed to encourage ordinary people like you, simply because we are ordinary people like you.

YOU

Yes, of course. This challenge extends to you, too. God wants to use you! Based on what you have read here, and hopefully tested by the scriptures in prayer, will you accept it?

> Jesus went through all the towns and villages, teaching in their synagogues, proclaiming the good news of the kingdom and healing every disease and illness. When he saw the crowds, he had compassion on them, because they were harassed and helpless, like sheep without a shepherd. Then he said to his disciples, 'The harvest is plentiful but the workers are few. Ask the Lord of the harvest, therefore, to **send out workers** into his harvest field.'
>
> (Matthew 9:35–38)

This is such an exciting ministry we are all being called into, to demonstrate the full gospel:

> As you go, proclaim this message: 'The kingdom of heaven has come near.' **Heal** those who are ill, raise the dead, cleanse those who have leprosy, drive out demons. Freely you have received; freely give.
>
> (Matthew 10:7–8)

What is more, it is so rewarding and enjoyable! What can be greater fun than to partner with God to minister His amazing grace to the people we meet every day?

> For the kingdom of God is not a matter of eating and drinking, but of righteousness, peace and **joy** in the Holy Spirit …
>
> (Romans 14:17)

I wonder if Francis of Assisi had the following scripture in mind when he famously sent out his monks with the instruction to preach the gospel but only to use words if necessary?

> For the kingdom of God is not a matter of talk but of **power**.
>
> (1 Corinthians 4:20)

NOTES

[1] The Bethel Sozo Ministry website includes this explanation of the meaning of the Greek word *sozo*.

[2] The influence of the teaching of Bill Johnson will be found throughout this book so I think it right to make a general acknowledgement here rather than to 'interrupt' the flow of the text in the many relevant places.

Chapter 8

■

HOPE, FAITH AND EXPECTANCY

You may ask me for anything in my name, and I will do it.

(John 14:14)

FAITH AND LOVE ARE THE ABSOLUTES of the Christian life. Love is to do with character, and faith with power. It would be true to say that faith is energised by love. These absolutes, exercised with compassion, are the foundations of the healing ministry, rather than just a desire to see results (or even to feed the ego).

Healing is only one of the issues we encounter as Christians where there is a clear progression in both our outlook and in the outcomes of our ministries. Invariably, we begin with **hope**, hoping that the person we minister to will be healed. Gradually, hope develops into **faith**, believing that the person will be healed. Eventually, faith becomes so strong that we have complete **expectation** for the person to be healed.

Some may consider the above to be too simplistic, but I honestly believe it to be an accurate assessment of how healing, and other, ministries develop. So, if you are a complete 'beginner' and what you have is best described as hope, rather than faith or expectation, press on and you will progress. You will probably also find that the rate of progression varies between the different types of healing needs presented before you.

I came across a picture on Facebook that really spoke to me about the difference between faith and expectation (expectant faith) and how the church across the world is simply not at one over this, at least in terms of healing today. The picture was a photograph of a parking sign for the disabled in a church car park. It had the usual line illustration of a wheelchair at the top but certainly not the regular slogan underneath. This sign confidently proclaims the words, 'Soon to be healed'. Isn't that wonderful? That's what I call expectancy of the highest level. But how many church leaders do you know who would happily display such a sign in the car park?

Some friends of mine have shared with me from a sermon they heard about praying for the sick. The preacher spoke about two kinds of faith. One is where you pray in hope that the person will be healed. The other is when you pray knowing that the person will be healed. The second one was linked with a specific word of knowledge having been received beforehand, the point being that this would raise faith. Could one method be right and the other wrong, or is that being too simplistic? Do you agree with that preacher? Should there be more options to consider?

As mentioned in Chapter 5, I remember during my early days as a Christian that it was not unusual to hear the words, 'if it be Thy will', tacked on to the end of prayers, especially when praying for the sick. The sick person was not usually present as there was rarely an opportunity taken to pray with them. I hope this issue has already been dealt with satisfactorily (see Chapter 5) and that we can accept that it is the will of God to heal the sick.

Faith is an attitude of the heart of a believer that is continually anticipating (expecting) what God is going to do. It is living from what cannot be seen towards what can be seen. It connects what is available from Heaven to the need that is to be met here on earth.

Experience and expectancy are closely linked, normally in direct proportion to one another. If our positive experience is limited, or non-existent, it is likely that our expectation of a positive, or 'successful', healing ministration will also be limited or non-existent. Conversely, if we have seen many people healed our expectation levels are more likely to be high. Not only does experience influence our expectations, it can also affect our theology. Many negative theologies, or mindsets, have been developed over the years to try to explain away negative 'results'.

On recent trips to Cali, Colombia, our friend Paul Bennison has taken with him a guy who is a professional builder. *Danny* went for the primary purpose of helping with a special building project for impoverished children in the city. He confessed that he had never prayed for the sick and had never seen a miracle, so he was happy to concentrate on the building work and just offer prayer support from the back during meetings in which healing would be ministered.

At the first church meeting he attended there, he was encouraged by Paul to try to join in with prayer for the sick, as many people had come forward. Reluctantly, he agreed, and the first person he faced was a lady who had been blind from birth and was severely arthritic!

This is a typical experience for those who travel with Paul for the first time. Not quite 'knowing what he was doing', Danny offered up his best prayer, in **hope**. Within three minutes, the lady had full vision restored and was pain free as far as arthritis was concerned. Immediately, Danny had moved from hope to **faith** and, after three more trips to Cali, on to **expectancy**.

You may have heard of theological concepts such as *dispensationalism* and *cessationism*. Adherents believe that the gifts of Holy Spirit were no longer required after either the early apostolic era, in the first century AD, or after the canon of scripture was completed, in the fourth century AD.

I would suggest that these views are based upon a lack of positive healing experience,[1] not upon an accurate interpretation of scripture. To put it bluntly, if we expect nothing, we should not be disappointed if that is what we receive! I have heard it said that, in the Kingdom environment, what we expect will be drawn to us. Or, to put it another way, we will attract what we expect. Holy Spirit expects the impossible of us because He gives us the capacity to do the impossible.

I believe that the Bible gives us every reason to be positively expectant and that God is ready, willing and able to do more than we can ask or imagine (Ephesians 3:20). Let us 'taste and see that the LORD is good' (Psalm 34:8). Hebrews 6:12 tells us that 'through faith and patience [we] inherit what has been promised'. This speaks of *abiding* faith, and people with abiding faith seem to attract more promises into their lives than those without it.

One of the first 'obstacles' we need to deal with is the idea of a 'degree of difficulty' in respect of different varieties of dis-ease, sickness or injury. From a purely medical or surgical point of view this does make sense. Not so from a heavenly perspective. God's healing power is so awesome that a brain tumour is not a bigger problem to Him than a straightforward headache.

As we are totally dependent upon the power of God for healing of any kind, we should not let ourselves be 'put off' by whatever ailment the person in front of us is suffering from. I know, from my own experience, that is easier said than done, but we must resolve to press on towards that goal, trusting that the Lord sets us up to succeed rather than to fail. There is no sickness of any kind in Heaven and our goal is to bring more of Heaven to earth, as Jesus did (see the Lord's Prayer).

There should be some tangible evidence of our faith and/or expectation present when we minister. As a person gains experience of healing ministry, it is possible that they will find that certain things seem to be healed quickly and easily, while there is no apparent 'success' with some others.

I have found this to be so with skeletal issues to the point where I become excited, not worried, by what might happen when I minister. From the early days, when Cathy and I encountered a lady with long-lasting effects from whiplash, it has been noticed, by others as well as ourselves, that people with these problems are practically always healed when we minister to them. However, I must emphasise that is not because we are 'special' people – it is always down to Him.

The 'growing out of arms and/or legs' is a case in point as we have watched God do such things many times now. I must be honest and say that the very first person we ministered to, who was born with one leg shorter than the other, was *not* healed at the time, so perseverance was essential.

I was on a ministry trip to India in October 2015 and it was noticeable that *Ravi*, one of the pastors who hosted Phil and me, walked with a pronounced limp. He explained that he had been involved in a motorcycle accident about ten years previously and the resultant operation to set the bone had left him with the damaged leg almost an inch shorter than the other one. This is not unusual if someone has had an operation to repair a fracture.

Ravi sat on a straight-backed chair, removed his shoes and socks, stretched out his legs and enabled me to hold them up by kneeling and placing my hands behind his heels. Although I must quickly add that this is not a scientifically accurate way of measuring legs and is therefore not credible in the eyes of the medical profession, it does give you a reasonable indication of what you are dealing with.

By placing your thumbs on the highest point of the (inside) ankle bones, while the feet are about 6 inches apart, then bringing the feet together, you get a fair idea of how much difference there is between the (apparent) lengths of each leg. If both your thumbs come together, knuckle exactly to knuckle, there is no obvious difference. In this instance, the centres of my thumb knuckles were almost an inch apart, which confirmed what Ravi had told us.

It was then a matter of taking authority, in the name of Jesus, trusting in the power of Holy Spirit, and commanding the skeleton to realign. The 'growth', a creative miracle on this occasion, began almost instantly. His legs became perfectly matched, length-wise, in no more than a minute or so. Praise God!

To see with your own eyes such growth and/or adjustment is an incredible faith-builder for all who witness it. Therefore, as Eagles 4031, we will always use this type of ministry as a demonstration of healing in our workshop teaching sessions. However, we make a point of explaining that such 'measuring' is neither scientifically accurate nor medically accepted practice.

Some will perhaps mistake it for arrogance when I say that my expectancy level, when faced with cases like this, is so high now that it is almost as if faith is not necessary. But, of course, faith is a vital ingredient of expectancy and it really is present! There is simply a marked absence of self-imposed pressure.

Faith is a gift and healing is a grace, so I know I have nothing to take personal pride in when these things happen. The glory is all the Lord's and so it should be. However, there are plenty of other situations in which I find that my levels of expectant faith are nowhere near as high. That is a failing on my part, not

God's, and I am constantly seeking to address it as I learn and
grow in this ministry. As an example, I have now seen scoliosis
healed several times whereas there was no obvious 'success' with
the first few people I encountered who had this condition of the
spine.

There is always a possibility of our faith being 'tested' by
God. His intent in this will always be for a positive outcome. Such
testing is solely intended to equip us to succeed, not to put us under
pressure, or make us feel inadequate or under condemnation.

Being part of a ministry team is always a good thing but,
as you can imagine, the team comes into its own when different
members find that they seem to have a special 'anointing' for the
healing of specific problems. While nobody wants to be considered
a 'specialist' in any area, to have complementary 'anointing' among
the members of a team is a great asset. As we minister alongside
one another and see people healed of ailments that we ourselves
have had no previous 'success' with, our faith grows, and our
experience expands.

I don't want to leave the subject of faith without referring
to the 'gift of faith', listed in 1 Corinthians 12. Now, as already
mentioned, all faith is a gift from God. But, when we think about
faith, we normally do so in the context of our faith being *in* God.
However, as Randy Clark teaches well,[2] there is also what can be
called the faith *of* God. When this is granted to us, I believe we
are experiencing the 'gift of faith' as described in 1 Corinthians
12:9. The gift of faith comes to increase our current level of faith
so that the need of the moment will be met. The thinking behind
this is that the breakthrough would not have occurred in response
to our usual level of faith.

We find the same use of language in Galatians 2:20, where a
strictly accurate translation of the Greek would render a certain
phrase as 'I live by the faith **of** the Son of God'. The best way to

describe this gift of 'the faith of God' would be a knowing, with absolute certainty, with total confidence, that God will do exactly what He has placed on our hearts.

When you have total conviction (i.e. an unwavering certainty and expectation) that God is going to do a particular thing, you begin to find that you have the courage to *decree* the will of God in a matter. In the absence of such conviction, you can only *ask* Him to do it (prayer). I believe He longs to see that progression in each one of us.

Returning to the subject of anointing, I was advised, right from the beginning, to go where the anointing is and trust the Lord to pour more of it into me! This may seem flippant to some, but I am deadly serious about it. So, I take every possible opportunity to attend meetings and conferences where healing will be ministered, just to be there and literally absorb everything God wants to give me. If you like, I am looking to 'catch' whatever the anointed minister is 'leaking' ('overflowing' from them), or specifically offering by way of a prayer of impartation.

One of the best ways of doing this is to volunteer to be a 'catcher' for the prayer line. In case this term is one you are not familiar with, a 'catcher' is a person who stands behind someone receiving ministry to break their fall, if they go down in the Spirit,[3] to gently lower them to the floor. (Incidentally, a thoughtful ministry will have some 'modesty cloths' available, especially for ladies who fall, to preserve their dignity if they are wearing skirts or dresses rather than trousers or leggings.)

Cathy and I have been part of the ministry team for the Healing Centre, which is run by Eastgate church, since it began in January 2012. In that time, there have been a growing number of remarkable healing testimonies involving a very wide variety of things, including several types of cancer.

The team always spends at least an hour worshipping and sharing encouraging testimonies before the doors are opened to the public. This takes us into the presence of God and lifts our faith for what lies ahead. At the end, we have a feedback time to share testimonies from that morning, which we celebrate and give glory to God for together. The more we see and hear about God's healing grace being manifested, the more our hope, faith or expectation levels rise. We find that the testimonies change our awareness of what can (and does) happen, by the grace of God.

'If we do not live a life of miracles (healing and otherwise), God does not get all the glory He is due,' says Bill Johnson. God is glorified when we share with each other the stories of what we have seen Him do. And we discover that the expectation for Him to do it again grows.

There is an excellent book by Bill Johnson and Randy Clark, entitled *Healing: Unplugged*,[4] that I have found to be a huge encouragement and faith builder. The book is essentially the transcript from two occasions on which these gentlemen interviewed one another about their respective experiences over many years in the healing ministry.

God has taught them so much through one another during a long friendship and they have become great encouragers of each other when it comes to pressing into the 'more' of God. When one of them encounters problems with the healing of a certain sickness and the other has known breakthrough in that area, they learn from one another, under God, how to press in for that same breakthrough. Sometimes, achieving a great breakthrough will result only from a period of dedicated prayer and fasting.

Each one of us can learn from and be encouraged by what they share with one another. We can do the same things among our own friends and/or team members. All this builds faith and increases our levels of expectancy.

More recently, I have come across another picture on Facebook that moves on a stage from the one mentioned at the beginning of this chapter. On this sign, there is a wheelchair depicted on the right, and to the left of that is a person getting up out of the chair. Wow!

And, don't forget, the following is what Paul writes in Ephesians 3:20–21 to remind us that we can never be over-expectant about what God can and will do for us. Let your hope rise into faith and your faith into expectancy as you look to Him for the more that He wants to give both to and through you.

> Now to him who is able to do immeasurably more than all we ask or imagine, according to his power that is at work within **us**, to him be glory in the church and in Christ Jesus throughout all generations, for ever and ever! Amen.

Remember also that effective faith comes from rest, not from striving or effort. Maintaining a heart of rest, at peace in God, drawing on His presence, is vitally important in the area of faith and expectancy.

NOTES

[1] Please note that cessationists and dispensationalists have no expectation of any gifts of the Spirit being manifested, not just healing or miracles. Unbelief is faith in the inferior; it means being focused on what can be seen, on what is humanly possible, without divine intervention.

[2] Randy Clark, *The Healing Breakthrough* (Chosen Books, 2016) (see his chapter 17).

[3] For those not familiar with the expression and/or experience of 'going down in the Spirit', perhaps I should explain that sometimes the power of God the Holy Spirit comes upon a person in such a way that they fall

to the floor as though fainting, although remaining conscious. This is not something to be alarmed about; after all, we are talking about the God of Love being at work as He has chosen to act on such occasions. Some ministries have gained a reputation for pushing people over, a practice we are totally opposed to.

[4] Bill Johnson and Randy Clark, *Healing: Unplugged* (Chosen Books, 2012).

Chapter 9

———————■———————

DEALING WITH DISAPPOINTMENT

Therefore, since through God's mercy we have this ministry, we do not lose heart.

(2 Corinthians 4:1)

THE BOTTOM LINE FOR THE healing ministry is facilitating an encounter between the person seeking healing and the Presence of God. If someone I minister to is not healed then, for some reason, this connection has not been made. Yes, I will be disappointed but, more importantly, I need to resolve to grow in faith and assurance in that area by persistently pursuing breakthrough in it.

In November 2011, after I had experienced increasing discomfort in my left knee for a while, I was persuaded to consult my doctor for a diagnosis of the cause of this. He told me that the problem was with my hip so, thinking he had not heard me correctly, I repeated that the pain was in my knee. He is a friend so, smiling, he took my outstretched left leg in his hands and moved it sharply to my left. The resultant pain in my hip told me what I should have realised anyway: that he knew what he was talking about!

The anticipated problem was arthritis and I was sent to the hospital for both my hips to be X-rayed. When I saw my doctor after the results came through, it was confirmed that I had arthritis in both hips. On a scale of 1 to 10, my left hip was affected at a level of 5 and my right hip at 2. I could expect to need a left hip replacement operation within three years. *No chance*, thought I. Not now we know what to pray about, and certainly not after my healing experience with ME.

I was ministered to subsequently on many occasions, sometimes with an apparent improvement being the cause for much optimism and the resolve to press on to see the disease defeated. The last time I was prayed for was after a Sunday evening service the day before my operation was scheduled to take place. I received a brand-new titanium hip the following afternoon.

To say I was disappointed would be an understatement. Quite frankly, I felt that God had not only let me down but, even more importantly, His own good name as well! Learning to live with the mystery of why some people are healed and some are not will become an essential prerequisite of our healing ministries. And 'What do I do next?' is a more important question than 'Why?'

We must accept that we will not always be given the reason for apparent 'failure'. We are not owed an explanation by right. 'A living sacrifice has its head removed to give up the right to understand and/or to control' (Andy Mason). Augustine of Hippo said, 'If you understood it, it is not God.' Now, those statements may seem a bit extreme, but what I think both men are referring to is *complete* understanding. God is too big, and we are too small by comparison, for that to be possible in every situation, don't you agree?

We need the resolve and confidence in God to continue to believe what we have been believing and press on towards the goal – the 100% 'success' record that only Jesus has achieved to date. I am not going to pretend that this is easy, but I am going to say that it is important to be persistent and not to give up. Seeking peace when there is an absence of answers is important, trusting Him no matter what, drawing encouragement from our experiences of what God has done, not dwelling upon what He hasn't. God is good. That is His unchanging nature.

- 'There are times of great victory as well as times of difficult defeat – or at least what seems like defeat.'

- 'We don't take the credit when someone does get healed but neither do we take on any guilt, shame or condemnation if they don't.'

These wise words are from Randy Clark and I have heard similar sentiments expressed by various people in the healing ministry in recent years. Despite my own disappointing experience, I find them encouraging and I appreciate why we need to take them to heart if we are to resist the temptation to give up that often comes after apparent 'failure'. Well, we know who is the source of that sort of temptation, don't we?

I remember hearing Bill Johnson say that it is vitally important for our disappointments to be brought before God for healing. Failure to do this means they will fester and surface at some time in the future. 'Exalt Him in the area where disappointment has been suffered,' he says, 'and praise Him for who He is.' Feed on promises, prophecies and scriptures that encourage us and build us up again. Bill has also said that we will get breakthrough when we have experienced disappointment, provided the disappointment/'failure' is not permitted to deter us. We won't get it right unless we are prepared to accept that we may get it wrong sometimes.

There can be lots of reasons why someone is not healed that have nothing to do with the level of faith of the person ministering. Those reasons may or may not be revealed to us. If they are not, then it can be a cause for more disappointment that we will need to overcome if we are to pursue our calling to heal the sick.

Jenny Lake, first wife of John G. Lake, was greatly used by God in, or rather after, meetings her husband held in South Africa in the early years of the twentieth century. Lake's ministry was powerfully anointed, and many sick people were healed. He went against the usual practice of the day and ushered those who were *not* healed into a separate room after the meeting.

His wife would then enter the room and, by means of revelation, words/messages of knowledge or wisdom, Holy Spirit would invariably reveal to her the reason why each person had not been healed. This could be due to unforgiveness, bitterness or resentment on their part, or other similar obstacles that the enemy would use to try to thwart the redemptive purposes of God.

If the person responded positively to the revelation, the situation was dealt with and then they were ministered to again. Much rejoicing ensued when they found that they were healed this time. Those who were not prepared to respond positively to the revelation were told that there was nothing further that could be done for them and they were free to leave. If only it could be like this in every meeting that you and I attend!

Sometimes, there will be breakthrough, often due to a word of knowledge. Other times, as in the case of my hip, we are none the wiser. Coming to terms with the realisation that Almighty God is not bound to explain everything to you or me every time is another difficulty to be overcome. I have learned that we should not 'require' explanations from Him. Our help comes from Presence, not from principles, as Kris Vallotton teaches.

I do know that, in my case, I had become increasingly inclined to dismiss medical or surgical treatment in favour of healing by divine intervention every time. It is just possible that I went through the operation so that I would gain a renewed appreciation of the medical profession and understand that dedicated doctors and nurses are used by God as one method of healing. They are particularly essential when there are no believers around to minister to the patients!

I can accept that rebuke because there are several qualified medical practitioners in the Eastgate environment who believe passionately in both aspects of healing. Indeed, one of them (Pete Carter) has said that, 'Medicine is directly in line with God's will because it seeks to eradicate sickness and there is no sickness in Heaven.'

Another possibility that I am considering is that it is essential for me to put my pursuit of God, purely for Himself, above my pursuit of His gifts and His blessings, of what He can do for me (or through me). In that case, my love for and dedication to Him should not be affected in any way by my life experiences. If Jesus Christ is the same yesterday, today and forever (Hebrews 13:8), that is true whatever the circumstances of my life are, positive or negative. Faith and trust far outweigh complete understanding.

To some, this may seem a bit harsh, but I am not so sure. Often, we gain more from the difficult lessons than we do from the relatively easy ones. The fact is, 'God is good', no matter what, and He loves me with an everlasting love, no matter what. So, I am learning to live with the 'mystery' and to press on.

One of my great disappointments of recent times concerns *Adam*, a friend who has had an eye removed because of a tumour behind it, followed barely 12 months later by major heart surgery. This is a man who is very much involved in the healing ministry, among other (Christian) spiritual pursuits, and has seen the hand of God at work on many occasions.

Adam has recovered well, says he feels better than he has done for years, and has simply carried on where he left off, after submitting to the NHS. My point is that, although many people prayed for him before the surgeons could get near him, his physical healing was provided through the medical profession.

God rewards our obedience rather than our performance. Sometimes our tentative 'Excuse me' as we open up a healing conversation with a stranger is more important than a 'successful' outcome. God has it all in hand anyway and could have someone else lined up to minister the required healing at another, more appropriate time. It is not all about me, is it? He has all sorts of ways of working everything together for good that we may never be party to. Just trust Him (by faith, not by sight).

It is interesting to observe the number of times that people who receive healing ministry, without an obvious positive result at the time, express gratitude for the love and compassion expressed in the ministry. I am also inclined to believe those who maintain that, when we pray, it is impossible for God to do nothing. Somehow, whether it is readily apparent or not, a blessing of some kind is always imparted.

Cathy had two experiences of offering to pray for non-Christian colleagues on different occasions when she was still working as a school teacher. She really stepped out in faith, but neither was healed, and in fact, both subsequently had to take a few days off sick! Cathy was both disappointed and dreading their return to work and her first conversation with them. But both told her how grateful they were for her loving concern.

Later, when Cathy was feeling unwell, one of them offered to pray for her! She didn't know the 'right' words to say, so Cathy encouraged her to be herself. She was not instantly healed but felt the warmth of God's presence in the part of her body that was dis-eased. Oh, sweet mystery!

Believing that God can heal is intellectual faith and is not at all the same as believing that He will heal, there and then. If what we have is intellectual faith, then it is more likely that we will encounter disappointment, for it is not the kind of faith with which we please God (Hebrews 11:6). It is belief in a concept rather than faith in a Person. It is a degree of *belief* in a God who *is*, but it is not *faith* in a God who *does*. There is no expectancy involved.

Prayers of this kind will probably end with something like so many that I remember from my early days as a Christian: 'if it be Thy will'. In those days, I became pretty much convinced that this was the template for all praying! When nothing seems to happen in response to such prayers, that 'nothing' is interpreted as being the will of God. Of course, even if the person who says this means well, they will still be disappointed, so I am not trying to belittle anyone. But it's not expectant faith, is it?

Now faith is confidence in what we hope for and assurance about what we do not see.

(Hebrews 11:1)

Smith Wigglesworth's regular exhortation from the pulpit was
'Only believe!', taken from Mark 5:36 and the raising of Jairus'
daughter:

> As soon as Jesus heard the word that was spoken, he
> saith unto the ruler of the synagogue, Be not afraid, **only
> believe**.

(KJV)

If you know anything of Wigglesworth's story, then you know he
practised what he preached.

But even he was beset by kidney stone problems and experienced agony over several years until they were all passed by painful,
natural means. This often happened during meetings, so he had
to excuse himself temporarily. It is probably also as well to note
that he had made a vow some years before, when miraculously
healed from appendicitis that was expected to take his life, that
no surgeon's knife would ever cut him. Therefore, it was not his
practice to seek professional medical help!

OVERCOMING DISAPPOINTMENT

How do we overcome disappointment? This is not only a question
we need to ask ourselves but also one we should make every effort in
pursuing an answer to. That answer may be different for each one
of us but there will be areas of common ground and the common
denominator for most of them will be a misunderstanding of our
identity in Christ. Indeed, most of our limits and restrictions are
self-imposed.

If we take on board Paul's exhortation to be (being) filled with
the Spirit (Ephesians 5:18), it is worth remembering that only an
empty tin can is crushable, not a full one. The following verses are
also very encouraging:

> But we have this treasure in jars of clay to show that this all-surpassing power is from God and not from us. We are hard pressed on every side, but not crushed; perplexed, but not in despair; persecuted, but not abandoned; struck down, but not destroyed.

(2 Corinthians 4:7–9)

Let us remind ourselves again that God is good – always. Remember that He loves us with an everlasting, unconditional love. Don't forget that He never changes (Hebrews 13:8). Whatever our circumstances may be, whatever we may be encountering, He is God. He knows the end from the beginning. He works everything together for good (Romans 8:28). He loves us and always has our best interests at heart. There are times when a parent (e.g. a father) does, purely out of love, things that a child cannot understand and which, at the time, seem unfair, unreasonable and even wrong to the child, when they are filtered through their own comparatively limited understanding and experience.

Our Father knows us better than we know ourselves. Character building is a heavenly priority and, often, we learn more and mature more quickly through adversity. Nothing is wasted in Heaven's economy. We can become over-confident, *self*-confident, when we are successful, when everything always turns out well all the time. If we are to be trusted by God with a greater measure of 'success' then we must develop the character to handle it well. True faith is focused on Him, not on *self*-anything.

No successful person will have *never* experienced 'failure'. Indeed, such failures can probably be considered an essential part of the recipe for ultimate 'success'. It was Winston Churchill who said, 'Success is moving from failure to failure without losing enthusiasm.' That is persistence!

If we are able-bodied, and we want to walk from A to B we do not give undue thought to the ease with which we can get up out of a chair and do just that. It is entirely natural to us. But that was not always true of us. As a baby developing into a toddler we had to learn to walk, and the only way was by trial and error. Every time we tripped and tumbled our parents would, without criticising, pick us up, comfort us and encourage us to try again. This scenario would be repeated time and time again until walking came as naturally to us as breathing.

My point is that the same principle applies to our walk with the Lord. At first, we may stumble and fall a few times, make mistakes and get it wrong. Even so, our Father is not standing beside us and scolding us. He is there, just loving us and encouraging us all the time. With persistence and determination, we will get there in the end, learning valuable lessons along the way.

During the learning process, all cyclists fall off their bikes occasionally, or horse riders fall from their mounts from time to time. The important thing is to get back in the saddle again as quickly as possible, pressing on towards the goal (Philippians 3:12). The writer to the Hebrews tells us that there is a whole 'cloud of witnesses' cheering us on from Heaven. Persistent prayer brings in God's purposes that are already ordained.

If we are aiming for the best, with the best of intentions and a good heart, there will still be occasions when disappointment must be dealt with but let us not be discouraged by them. It has been said that 'our calling is in our conquering'. Muscles are built up by meeting resistance, so treat your faith as a muscle to be developed by exercising it regularly.

Steve Backlund offers some wise words: 'He who says he can and he who says he can't are both right. Who do you say you are? Are you and I who our experiences say we are, or are we who God says we are?'

Again, we find how important it is to know our **identity** in Christ and to live out of that truth, from Heaven (i.e. seated in heavenly places) to earth.

> Since through God's mercy we have this ministry, we do not lose heart.
>
> (2 Corinthians 4:1)

> The things that mark an apostle – signs, wonders and miracles – were done among you with great perseverance.
>
> (2 Corinthians 12:12, NIV 1984)

Chapter 10

---■---

DEALING WITH OPPOSITION

For our struggle is not against flesh and blood ... but against the authorities, against the powers of this dark world and against the spiritual forces of evil in the heavenly realms.

(Ephesians 6:12)

ONE THING WE CAN BE SURE of when we step out in faith in any new venture for the Lord is that we will be opposed. We have an enemy who hates any such activity and the potential of it, so please don't be surprised if you come across evidence of his hatred, both of you and of what you are seeking to do. Healing the sick is like raiding his trophy cabinet, a constant reminder to him of his once and forever defeat by Jesus, through His death and resurrection.

People will oppose us too, sometimes deliberately, sometimes unwittingly, and it is not unusual for there to be fellow believers among them. Jesus said, 'Whoever is not for me is against me'

(Matthew 12:30), so an opponent need only be someone who does not see things the same way, for example a person who does not believe that God heals today and that He wants to use people like you and me as His co-workers.

There will be believers who have experienced the disappointment of a loved one being sick, or even dying, despite having been prayed for both earnestly and sincerely. It is so easy for that level of disappointment to be channelled into opposition and for someone to be doing the enemy's work for him, albeit not deliberately. We need to be aware of the many negative possibilities and ask the Lord to upgrade our level of spiritual discernment.

The very existence of death and sickness is evidence of this high level of spiritual opposition to anything relating to the Kingdom of God. It was exactly this opposition that Jesus came to overcome.

> The reason the Son of God appeared was to destroy the devil's work.
>
> (1 John 3:8b)

> God anointed Jesus of Nazareth with the Holy Spirit and power, and ... he went around doing good and healing all who were under the power of the devil, because God was with him.
>
> (Acts 10:38)

The enemy wants us to be a victim, because it is then always someone else's fault. Instead, as the old song advises, we need to pick ourselves up, dust ourselves off, and start all over again.

You will recall from the testimony of my own healing (described in Chapter 1) that what had to be defeated was the spirit of infirmity. Now I do not subscribe to the theory that every sickness is specifically demonic in origin, but I do believe that, but for the Fall, there would be no sickness whatsoever. I would say that all sickness is at least attributable to the devil's original intervention in the affairs of mankind.[1]

It is commonly agreed that the purpose of the devil is to keep mankind from coming into a restored relationship with God. And, if or when that fails, his alternative strategy is to do everything possible to prevent Christians from becoming effective, fruitful children of God who are doing the works of Jesus. One way of achieving that, with many, is to afflict them with sickness.

Sometimes we provide him with opportunities by what we think, do or say: by sins of omission or commission, if you like. There are those who will interpret sickness, in this context, as a punishment from God. My response to that view is that it does not fit the character of the loving Father I have come to know. His purpose is to save us, not to condemn or afflict us. Most of us can quote John 3:16 but how many can recite verse 17 just as well?

Some will ask why God does not always protect us, to which I would reply that we cannot expect protection if, on occasion, our wilful actions conflict with His wishes and take us away from His shield of protection.

There are also times when the enemy just seems to slip in under the radar, without any provocation or invitation from us. I believe that is what happened to me with the spirit of infirmity and ME. In my case, it sneaked in under cover of an illness. With others, it will take advantage of a traumatic event. This was true of the persons with ME that God has graciously used us to minister healing to. As a result, those healings had to involve deliverance.

To take just two examples: one was a young lady who had been raped; the other was involved in a serious car accident for which she had blamed herself. Let me share with you what I remember of the latter's story.

We were on ministry team at the end of a meeting in which an appeal was made and many came forward for ministry in response. *Susie* was one of those. As it turned out, she was not responding specifically to that appeal. This was the only evening of the week of meetings when she could be in attendance and she was simply desperate for God to help her.

Cathy found her lying on the floor, slain in the Spirit, just a few feet from the platform. When it seemed appropriate, Cathy introduced herself and asked what the problem was. She was told it was ME, so she sent a message to get me to come over to help (applying the 'freely you have received, freely give' principle).

When I heard that Susie had ME, I suspected a spirit of infirmity could possibly be involved, as in my case. If so, it would be necessary to try to ascertain when it could have gained access to her life. I asked her how long she had suffered the symptoms of ME and she told me that it was for about 20 years. She was in her teens when the problem took hold. Then I asked her if anything significant had happened in her life just before the symptoms manifested. I was interested to find out if there had been any illness or traumatic event around that time. It was then that she told us about the car accident.

Apparently, Susie was driving at the time of the crash and her father was in the passenger seat. He was badly injured, but she escaped comparatively unscathed (at least physically). She felt total responsibility for her dad's injuries even though the accident was the fault of the other driver. We asked her if she had forgiven that person. I seem to recall that she thought she had but was happy to do so again, just in case that position of forgiveness had not been maintained. (Please note: forgiveness begins as a *choice*, not a feeling.)

We explained that, in our experience to date, ME was usually due to a spirit of infirmity gaining access to a body through illness or trauma and, with her permission, that is how we proposed to deal with her problem. She agreed to this and we then explained that unforgiveness could provide a landing ground, or 'welcome mat', for the enemy and we intended to take any such ground away. (Please note: I am not saying there is always a demonic root.)

That was done and then we asked her if she had forgiven herself. As a Christian, she knew that the blood of Jesus had obtained for her forgiveness from God, but it did not seem to occur to her that she could still be bound, to some degree, if she had not forgiven herself for what she still carried guilt about (her father's suffering, for example).

Once Susie appreciated that this could be another stronghold of the enemy, she readily agreed to co-operate, and, with a little prompting, she got through this part also in a prayerful way. Having satisfied ourselves that there were no other potential obstacles to her healing/freedom, we told her that it was now time to tell the demon to go. We also assured her that, having taken the ground away, it no longer had any 'rights' of occupancy to cling to.

She accepted this and, as she had been throughout, she remained totally co-operative. Clearly, she was very spiritually aware. This became more apparent when, after we took authority over the oppressor, in Jesus' name, and commanded it to go, she told us that it had moved but it was now on her back. Neither Cathy nor I could 'see' it but, for the reasons given above, we accepted Susie's word, simply and quietly reiterating our instruction to the demon to go because it had no grounds for disobedience to the command made in Jesus' name, backed up by the authority that He has delegated to us.

Immediately, Susie let out a joyful cry of freedom and, on her knees, she worshipped the One who had gloriously set her free. She thanked us, and we said our farewells, leaving her praising God. The sight of Susie lost in worship like that is something that will remain engraved on my memory – glory to God!

We first encountered *Laura* during another hectic time of ministry at the end of a conference in the same venue but the following year. She came to our attention originally because she was on the ground, screaming and causing a bit of a scene. *Rose*, one of the very experienced team leaders, got to her before I did.

This was fortuitous because I learned something valuable from how she dealt with the situation. The noise Laura was making caused most of us to assume that what we were hearing was a consequence of demonic manifestation. But Rose subsequently told us that this was not so; rather it was a matter of deep-seated emotional pain being released.[2]

Nevertheless, and this is one of the important lessons I learned from this initial encounter, Laura was told, quietly but firmly, that she had the authority to control what was happening and that she did not have to make that noise. As soon as she understood and processed that information she fell quiet.

What I learned was that a person not only has authority over the way they express their pain but also over a manifesting demon. This has proved invaluable in subsequent encounters, even one that same evening less than five minutes later! I applied the lesson I had just received, and the person concerned became quiet immediately, enabling those who were already ministering to her to proceed unhindered. (Please note: we can always learn from others.)

In case you have doubts about the authority we carry over the demonic, even while we are demonically oppressed ourselves, please remember that the Gadarene demoniac could run to Jesus and worship Him unhindered even before he was set free! He made the right choice and, in exercising his will to choose, could carry it through to the most amazing conclusion, by the grace of God. The enemy only has control insofar as we come into **agreement** with him, either knowingly or through ignorance.

Another common problem, which can have a demonic root, is rejection. Even if the problem does not begin with demonic oppression, if a person keeps giving ground to it, it is relatively easy for a demon of rejection to take advantage and set up 'home'. It is not unusual for a person to have no idea that they now have an oppressive companion because the demon can work to good effect without ever needing or wanting to draw attention to its presence.

Many years ago, I was having a time of ministry with a couple who were the leaders of the ministry team I was part of at the time. It was common practice to minister to one another occasionally to ensure that we were all 'OK' and best able to minister to others.

On this occasion, *Len* gently suggested to me that he thought I might have a problem with rejection. Apart from Holy Spirit giving a word of knowledge, I have no idea what could have prompted him to say this. In all honesty, I did not believe that this was true of me and told him so. Being a wise man, he didn't put pressure on me and moved on to something else.

A few days later, I was visiting a relative's home for Sunday lunch and, during the afternoon, my hostess pointed out a cassette she had just obtained. It was of Derek Prince teaching about spiritual warfare. I expressed interest in hearing it sometime and was firmly persuaded to take it away with me that day and to bring it back when I had finished with it.

Soon afterwards, sitting on my bed with notepaper and pencil to hand, I switched on the recording. Derek Prince was a great Bible teacher, also active in healing and deliverance ministry, so I was very interested in all he had to say, especially when he raised the subject of 'rejection'.

He taught that something like 80% of us suffer with this problem to some degree, whether Christian or not. He then went on to list the many symptoms of 'rejection' he was aware of. Much to my astonishment, I found myself mentally 'ticking off' quite a few of them! You can be sure that I was soon back in touch with Len to arrange another appointment!

To cut a longer story short, the roots of this 'infection' were traced back in time and a demon of rejection was expelled. This does not mean that I am immune to the temptation to feel rejected or that, without me exercising determination not to be susceptible, I am never going to become a victim again. I have learned to recognise the signs and to stand firmly on the ground of my freedom in Jesus so that I need no longer fall foul of that problem. This is what is known as 'walking out our healing'.

Anyone who is ministered to for healing and/or deliverance should be taught to 'walk out' their healing (or deliverance) as it is vitally important to be on guard against any attempt of the enemy to return and try to occupy old ground. If he can, he will (see Matthew 12:43–45). But we stand on the solid ground of the victory of Jesus over both sickness and the enemy and need not give an inch!

In Chapter 1, I described the remarkable healing (and deliverance) I received to be set free from ME (chronic fatigue). Now let me share with you what happened to me about a year after that great evening.

Cathy and I were having a new kitchen installed at home and the friend responsible for carrying out the work said he wanted to order a 'skip' to be parked at our house over a weekend so that the accumulated rubbish, principally the old kitchen units, could be put in it for removal and disposal by the skip hire company.

I asked him to order a slightly larger skip than he needed so that there would be room for the remains of a garden shed that we wanted to demolish. He agreed, and the skip was delivered. It was to be taken away again on the following Monday morning, which meant that our itinerary only left me Sunday morning to get the demolition done (we could go to church in the evening, which was our custom at the time anyway).

When I woke up that Sunday morning I felt all the old symptoms of ME at least as badly as I had ever experienced them before! There was no way that I could demolish a shed feeling like that. I am sure that God spoke in my spirit again because a thought immediately occurred to me: *Wait a minute! I'm healed. That is the truth, so what I'm feeling is a lie. I refuse to accept these symptoms as real. The shed is coming down!*

Still feeling very rough, I went out into the garden and faced the task before me. As soon as I grabbed the first heavy tool I needed and started work, all the symptoms disappeared, and I completed the job in good time with no ill effects. So, I have my own unforgettable experience of 'walking out my healing' in defiance of the attempts of the enemy to undermine what God had done.

For this reason, I am careful to advise the people I minister to, when appropriate, to be on guard against the enemy trying to return in some way. I advise them to stand on the truth, the reality of their healing (or deliverance), and not to give in to the 'father of lies' (John 8:44). Let me say it again: the enemy has authority over us only to the extent that we come into agreement with him.

The opposition we will face usually comes under one or more of four main headings: Discouragement; Fear; Frustration; and Accusation. Let us look very briefly at each of those.

DISCOURAGEMENT

What this means, literally, is to take one's courage away, and it will often accompany disappointment (see Chapter 9). *Dis*couragement is overcome by *en*couragement, which is why it is always a good idea to start our meetings with encouragement; by listening to healing testimonies, for example.

When we are alone it is our responsibility to encourage ourselves. We can do this by remembering things that God has already done in, for or through us. This is what we see exemplified so often in the Psalms.

Please do not be fooled into thinking that it is expressing humility to deflect any encouragement that comes our way. In fact, it is rather stupid to do this. If we remember to whom the glory truly goes (when we are alone with God afterwards) it is not wrong to accept thanks and encouragement from those who have appreciated the part we have played in their healing, or whatever it may be. We can all learn how to receive genuine encouragement without letting it go to our heads. After all, we are God's *co*-workers, aren't we?

If we are regularly tempted to be discouraged, then it is likely that the enemy has detected a vulnerability and is seeking to exploit it. Remember that he is a defeated enemy and rest on the victory of Jesus, and who you are in Christ. Then you can, and will, effectively resist such temptations.

FEAR

This is something that needs to be resisted or, if necessary, confronted. The enemy is always seeking an opening to undermine us, and fear is a tool he can be very effective with. We need to know where fear comes from. Paul reminds Timothy that it does not come from God:

> For God did not give us a spirit of timidity [fear], but a spirit of power, of love and of self-discipline [sound mind].

> (2 Timothy 1:7, NIV 1984)

We should also be wary of trying to justify our fears and anxieties, because sympathy does not alleviate fear. To all intents and purposes, it agrees with it! Instead it is driven out by love, so go to Jesus who is Love.

> There is no fear in love. But perfect love drives out fear, because fear has to do with punishment. The one who fears is not made perfect in love.
>
> (1 John 4:18)

FRUSTRATION

Delay is normally at the root of this one, especially if it involves healing. It is overcome by patience, which is a fruit of the Spirit (Galatians 5:22). Sharing, or recalling, testimonies is a good way of building faith and forbearance (the NIV alternative word for 'patience'). Frustration can also be linked with selfishness, especially if we are tempted to sink into the 'it's all about me' obsession, so prevalent in society today.

ACCUSATION

The Bible uses two Greek words referring to one who accuses:

- *Kategoros* describes a prosecutor, or plaintiff in a lawsuit, or one who speaks in a derogatory way of another. It occurs in Acts 23:30 and 35, Acts 25:16 and 18, and Revelation 12:10.

- *Diabolos* means adversary or enemy and is rendered 'accuser' in the King James Version, for example in 2 Timothy 3:3 and Titus 2:3. In most cases the devil is being described, so there can be no doubt about where any accusation against us, as Christians, originates.

Understanding both our identity and our righteousness in Christ is vital to overcoming the enemy's accusations. The righteousness of Jesus, which has been 'credited' to us by grace, is not in any way tainted by sin because He has never sinned. Therefore, living in the light of this brings us assurance and gives us total protection against the accuser.

CAPTIVES AND PRISONERS

We find captives and prisoners referred to in Isaiah 61:1, part of the passage that Jesus read in the synagogue and which He applied to His own mission (see Luke 4:21).

At first sight, these two words may seem to be synonymous, but we should never make such assumptions without looking a little further, asking for the guidance of Holy Spirit, who 'leads us into all Truth' (see John 16:13). Both words refer to people who are bound, or confined, in some way, but do they have the same meaning? No matter how we interpret this, the same enemy provides the opposition.

Many people are held **captive** by something, but they have no idea that they are bound. My experience with rejection is one example. Captivity is opposition the enemy has imposed upon us, which holds us back from being all we are meant to be in Christ. People who are captive to something need help to be set free. The problem is that, if they do not know they are captives, they will be completely unaware that they are being deprived of freedom. Living in the wrong place for a long time can also make that place feel 'normal'. That 'normality' can then be accepted as 'the way it is' with no hope or expectation for change.

Often, the only way we can really help such people is by receiving revelation from Holy Spirit that the problem exists (as Len did in my case with rejection). We need this revelation in order to be made aware of the problem the person has, but that does not mean we can immediately leap into 'ministry mode' to set them free. You will recall that Len shared with me what he believed the Lord had told him, but he was very sensitive in holding back when I was unable to respond positively to the disclosure.

Just as I did, all captives also need revelation from God to realise that they have a problem. Only then are they able to seek help to be set free. If or when we minister through words of knowledge, we may encounter a situation that is revealed to us but is not responded to. There are times when, as part of the revelation, we are made aware who it is who has the problem. But we need to be sensitive, to hold back until they come into an awareness of the matter for themselves. Failing to respond does not automatically mean that they are in denial. That is another issue entirely.

Those who are held as **prisoners** by the enemy are different in that they usually know they have a problem; a compulsion to view pornography is a common one. Some will truly want to be set free, but that does not mean it will not be a struggle for them. Some will deny they have the problem even though they know they are being dishonest. The former will most likely seek ministry, the latter will not, even though you may know who they are by revelation. Such people cannot be helped until they change their minds, which is the essence of repentance. It is a matter of choice – for them.

'Prisoners' who come forward for ministry may do so early enough for it to be relatively simple and easy to set them free, following repentance and forgiving anyone who may have been involved in causing them to have the problem.

Others, especially if their problem has been long term, will have almost certainly opened themselves up to the demonic. Pursuing their habit, compulsion, or whatever the issue is that causes the problem, will have been like laying down a 'welcome mat' for demonic oppression.

If a demon is involved then the problem cannot be dealt with, the person cannot be set free, until it is expelled. Again, this will involve leading the person into sincere repentance and, if necessary, encouraging them to choose to forgive anyone who has contributed to them being in bondage. Then the 'ground' the enemy sits on 'legitimately' can be removed. Once that is done, we simply take authority over the demon in the name of Jesus and command it to leave. (Please note that **legalism** is very prevalent in the demonic realm.)

SUMMARY

Both Christians and non-Christians have a common enemy whose purpose is either to keep us from Christ or, if that fails, to stop us from being effective and fruitful Christians. If we are called into a specific Christian ministry, we can be certain that we will be challenged by an enemy who wants to discourage us, ideally to the point where we give up. In Luke 4 we read of this happening to Jesus after His baptism by John. So, we need to be aware, alert and on our guard against any form of opposition.

Conversely, if we do not experience some form of opposition, perhaps we should ask ourselves why this might be? One possible answer is that we are not doing anything to upset the enemy and cause him to want to oppose us. In other words, we are probably failing to pursue our role in the heavenly family business (see 1 John 3:8, for example).

Whatever kind of opposition we, or others, experience, we need to remember that the victory of Jesus is a once and forever victory and the only chance the enemy gets to overturn this (in us) is through any opportunity we give to him (by agreement).

So, let us be encouraged to do our level best to make sure he cannot find a chink in the armour of God we are given to wear

(Ephesians 6:11) and therefore is unable to oppose us successfully! It also helps to keep ourselves in a relationship with good, trusted Christian friends to whom we can make ourselves accountable if and when we have an issue to deal with.

NOTES

[1] We need to be careful in dealing with sickness, or other issues, involving both the demonic and non-Christians. The guideline we observe, when ministering to non-Christians, is not to move into deliverance unless either

1. the person has first made a commitment to Jesus, or is clearly going to do so, or
2. Holy Spirit very clearly leads us to move into deliverance.

This is because only a Christian has the protection of the indwelling Holy Spirit to guard against further attack(s). Christians need to be warned about this possibility and how to maintain effectively their healing/deliverance when it happens. Non-Christians, on the other hand, have no such protection and run the risk of further oppression once their 'house' has been swept clean (see Matthew 12:45).

[2] The following is the written testimony that Laura submitted following a ministry appointment we had arranged with her the day after the situation described earlier. It is used with permission, but we have withheld her true name. This gives a fair idea of the reason for the emotional pain she was releasing so dramatically. The ministry time did involve some forgiveness issues and deliverance as well as healing.

> Father, Jesus and Holy Spirit, you are amazing! After years of emotional turmoil, you have reminded me of the love you have for me, and that you can fill all the areas of love that I've expected people to fill but have been let down by [them].
>
> I have had chronic neuropathic pain for 21 years, which I have had healing for before, as well as ministry on a deep level.

Today, Holy Spirit realigned my pelvic area (I was told I would get six or seven sessions of expensive chiropractic treatment for free!). My body physically moved into quite an unusual position!

I also had scoliosis of the lower lumbar spine which Holy Spirit straightened up for me. My shoulders are more level now and, finally, my legs were measured for alignment. I watched my legs level out and realign!

Praise the Lord! I love you, Jesus!

Chapter 11

OPEN HEAVENS

*You shall see heaven open, and the angels of God ascending
and descending on the Son of Man.*

(John 1:51)

E VER SINCE I FIRST CAME ACROSS the term 'open heavens' it has intrigued me. So much so that I looked at it both through the scriptures and other sources and put together some notes, which eventually became a talk that seemed to be a perfect fit for a conference in France that I was asked to speak at in May 2015. The talk was illustrated by a PowerPoint presentation of various works of art that complemented the subject matter. Because I would need the help of a translator in France, I took the opportunity of a suitable speaking engagement in the UK to 'trial run' the material before crossing the Channel. This chapter is based on that talk.

Oh, that you would rend the heavens and come down ...

(Isaiah 64:1)

This is a heartfelt cry, a powerful and prophetic prayer with more than a hint of desperation in it. Clearly it was relevant to the circumstances of Isaiah's own day but, being prophetic, there was more to it than that. God sees the whole picture and has a bigger plan – for the salvation of the entire world. So, the prayer is essentially for another day and, of course, we find its fulfilment in Jesus.

To locate the first instance of an open heaven in the Bible we need to go back to Genesis 28:12–22 and the account of Jacob's life. He was sent away by his mother, Rebekah, to escape the wrath of his brother, Esau. You will recall that he had cheated Esau out of his birthright blessing as the firstborn of twin sons. Jacob was on his way to seek refuge with his uncle, Laban, when he lay down to sleep for the night. As he slept, with his head on a rock for a pillow (ouch!), the Lord gave him a dream:

> He had a dream in which he saw a **stairway** resting on the **earth,** with its top reaching to **heaven,** and the angels of God were ascending and descending on it. There above it stood the LORD, and he said: 'I am the LORD, the God of your father Abraham and the God of Isaac. I will give you and your descendants the land on which you are lying. Your descendants will be like the dust of the earth, and you will spread out to the west and to the east, to the north and to the south. All peoples on earth will be blessed through you and your offspring. I am with you and will watch over you wherever you go, and I will bring you back to this land. I will not leave you until I have done what I have promised you.'
>
> When Jacob awoke from his sleep, he thought, 'Surely **the LORD is in this place**, and I was not aware of it.' He was

afraid and said, 'How awesome is this place! This is none other than the **house of God**; this is the **gate of heaven**.'

Early the next morning Jacob took the stone he had placed under his head and set it up as a pillar and poured oil on top of it. He called that place Bethel, though the city used to be called Luz.

Then Jacob made a vow, saying, 'If God will be with me and will watch over me on this journey I am taking and will give me food to eat and clothes to wear so that I return safely to my father's household, then the LORD will be my God and this stone that I have set up as a pillar will be God's house, and of all that you give me I will give you a tenth.'

I have gone beyond my subject matter by quoting all the above verses, simply because of the significance of the dream to Jacob, the change it brought about in him, and the ramifications which come right down to the present day. As for the specific references to open heavens, these words and phrases have been highlighted in bold type.

Our primary focus is on a stairway (some translations say 'ladder') linking Heaven and earth, with angels ascending and descending upon it. I believe this is an illustration of angels on assignment, coming down from Heaven to do the Lord's bidding, often in answer to our prayers, and returning from earth when their task is completed.

There is no barrier, no obstruction, between Heaven and earth here. The way is completely *open*. God is at work and he is using His angels to carry out His purposes:

Are not all angels ministering spirits sent to serve those who will inherit salvation?

(Hebrews 1:14)

Fast forwarding into the New Testament we find that this picture, this image, is repeated but with a very important difference:

> Philip, like Andrew and Peter, was from the town of Bethsaida. Philip found Nathanael and told him, 'We have found the one Moses wrote about in the Law, and about whom the prophets also wrote – Jesus of Nazareth, the son of Joseph.'
>
> 'Nazareth! Can anything good come from there?' Nathanael asked. 'Come and see,' said Philip.
>
> When Jesus saw Nathanael approaching, he said of him, 'Here truly is an Israelite in whom there is no deceit.' 'How do you know me?' Nathanael asked. Jesus answered, 'I saw you while you were still under the fig-tree before Philip called you.' Then Nathanael declared, 'Rabbi, you are the Son of God; you are the king of Israel.'
>
> Jesus said, 'You believe because I told you I saw you under the fig-tree. You will see greater things than that.' He then added, 'Very truly I tell you, **you will see "heaven open**, and the angels of God ascending and descending" on the Son of Man.'
>
> (John 1:45–51)

The promise from Jesus to Nathanael was that he would see what Jacob saw in his dream, except that the angels would not be ascending and descending upon a stairway, or ladder, but upon the Son of Man, Jesus Himself.

I believe this shows us that Jesus, the Saviour of the world, is the bridge between Heaven and earth. He is the way to Heaven. He is the essential link through whom you and I can access Heaven and angels will be sent to serve us, those who inherit salvation (forgiveness, healing and deliverance)! This is an amazing picture of how the Kingdom of Heaven invades earth to destroy the works of the prince of this world (1 John 3:8; John 12:31; 14:30; 16:11; Ephesians 2:2).

When we read the Gospels, we find that Jesus invariably speaks of the Kingdom of Heaven ('heaven' in the singular) but the Old Testament often uses the plural, 'heavens', as in Isaiah 64:1, for example. From this we can deduce that, somehow, there must be more than one heaven. Some ancient Jewish writings apparently speak of seven heavens. In the scriptures, Paul writes about visiting the **third** heaven (2 Corinthians 12:2). So, taking the biblical view, prompted by Paul's inspired writing, it seems there are at least three heavens.

As my reading of scripture, at least, has not located reference to any more, I am happy to settle for there being three heavens. But what and where are they? I doubt there will be any dispute about the first heaven, which can only be what we can see – the vast area with stars and planets surrounding earth.

As already mentioned, Paul refers to the third heaven, in 2 Corinthians 12:2, and scholars tend to agree that the third heaven is God's domain, and that makes perfect sense to me. We find mention of the throne room of Heaven in Revelation 4 and many believers have testified to either being caught up into Heaven or having heavenly visions. That has not been my privilege, to date, but I am not going to rule out something testified to by reliable people just because it has not been part of my own personal experience and may not be before I breathe my last.

As God is omnipresent it is hard to imagine there being an actual location for Heaven. Such a place would have to be outside the universe as we know it, and outside of time, but the Kingdom of Heaven is also 'at hand'. So, perhaps, the third heaven may be better described as a dimension rather than a location? I don't know for sure. Maybe it is both/and rather than either/or? It is enough for me to believe in the existence of Heaven and to accept Paul's description of it as being the third heaven.

I suppose it must be even harder for most of us to grasp the concept of a second heaven and where that might be located. As far as many scholars are concerned it would be what we call outer space, a place rather than a dimension. But just how far out is the outer space that would not be part of the first heaven, as defined above? What about the generally unseen spiritual dimension? Could it be that? Where else might we find the 'prince of the power of the air' (Ephesians 2:2, KJV)? I think the book of Daniel could be helpful in trying to unravel this mystery for us:

> Then he continued, 'Do not be afraid, Daniel. Since the first day that you set your mind to gain understanding and to humble yourself before your God, your words were heard, and I have come in response to them. But the prince of the Persian kingdom resisted me twenty-one days. Then Michael, one of the chief princes, came to help me, because I was detained **there** with the king of Persia. Now I have come to explain to you what will happen to your people in the future, for the vision concerns a time yet to come.'

> (Daniel 10:12–14)

We read in this chapter that Daniel has fasted and prayed for some time before an angel from (the third) heaven visits him (on earth within the first heaven) with the answer to his petitions. This angel explains that Daniel's prayer was heard immediately but the angel was delayed in bringing the answer by the prince of Persia (a demonic principality with responsibility for that region) until the archangel Michael was despatched to assist him to overcome the opposition. This seems to me to be a graphic example of spiritual warfare in the heavenly realms.

Therefore, I am drawn towards viewing the second heaven as an unseen entity between the first and third heavens that is occupied by enemy troops.

> For our struggle is not against flesh and blood, but against the rulers, against the authorities, against the powers of this dark world and against the spiritual forces of evil in the **heavenly** realms.
>
> (Ephesians 6:12)

Once again, this makes me consider the second heaven to be more of a dimension than a physical place, not least because, in any normal circumstance, we cannot see it even though we can sense the reality of such occupants and their dark assignments on the earth.

I am not suggesting that solely enemy forces occupy the second heaven either. It could well be that this is the whole of the spiritual dimension that exists, largely undetected by the five natural human senses but accessible by some 'gifted' persons, Christian or otherwise.

Jesus tells us, in Matthew 10:7 that 'the kingdom of heaven has come near'. Other translations render this as 'the kingdom of heaven is at hand', indicating that it is close enough to reach out and touch it. When Heaven touches earth, in ministry of various kinds, then there is a blend of the first and third heavens releasing the power of God – in healing for example.

It seems the third heaven can be both a place, spiritually if not physically, and a dimension. Heaven is described in Revelation 4, for example, as though it is a place. At the same time, for us here on earth, it is also 'at hand'. God is omnipresent. He cannot be contained in any one place or location (1 Kings 8:27), and God is spirit (John 4:24).

It is also possible that angels on assignment from the third heaven pass through the second heaven (as in the Daniel passage) on their way to earth, which is within the first heaven. I am just providing food for thought, based on speculation rather than fact.

For the time being, at least until I am enlightened to the contrary, I am inclined to consider the second heaven to be a spiritual **dimension** where the enemy hierarchy is located and which they seek to operate as a barrier between the first and third heavens, between God and mankind.

Therefore, I am persuaded that we can experience an **open** heaven, or heavens, when that barrier is either temporarily or permanently removed. I also believe that such removal is possible over an individual (see examples to follow) or a location (e.g. as Jacob experienced at the place he renamed Bethel). What other examples of 'open heavens' do we have experience of or know something about?

I believe it is right to begin with examples from the Bible and the New Testament. In Matthew 3:13–17 we read about the baptism of Jesus in the Jordan by John the Baptist, an event that I believe brought into the earthly realm the answer to Isaiah's prayer.

Some will argue that his prayer was answered at Bethlehem by the Incarnation. I can easily understand why that view might be taken, but my own inclination is towards the baptism. Here Jesus sets an example for us, not only by submitting to water baptism but also by effectively receiving the baptism of Holy Spirit (the Dove descending and resting upon Him).

This underlines that Jesus, the Son of Man, had laid aside His divinity for the period that He was on earth as a man, so that He became as we are, except that He was without sin. As a man, to whom was given the Spirit without limit (John 3:34), He is the perfect example for us, living a life we can aspire to as Christians.[1] As Bill Johnson points out, if Jesus did all the things He did as

God, we would still be impressed but we could not hope to emulate Him. Remember, Jesus said that we will do even greater things than He did (John 14:12)!

I believe that Holy Spirit descending upon Jesus at His baptism is an example of an open heaven and, because the Spirit (Dove) remained, Jesus was constantly under an open heaven wherever He went. There was no demonic obstruction or interference, meaning that the resources of Heaven were released both to and through Him as He ministered throughout the three years or so that followed His baptism. While it is right for us to be in awe of Him and all that He accomplished as the Son of Man, we can also be genuinely excited about the possibilities available to us as the ones the Son of God is now sending out to do likewise (John 20:21).

Another classic example of an open heaven in the life of the Son of Man is found in Matthew 17:1–8, the account of the Transfiguration. Here we see Jesus glorified, presumably as He is now when seated at the right hand of the Father in (the third) heaven? We also find Moses and Elijah, two of the prophets who lived hundreds of years before this incident, with Jesus in similarly glorified bodies. Peter, James and John, three disciples who are very human, are present too. So how many different dimensions are represented in this one place in one moment of time?!

The Day of Pentecost, considered by many to be the birth of the Christian church, is another example of an open heaven, which we find described in Acts 2. Some teach that the wind and flames are angels. Others would say that the birth of the church is described in John 20:22, when Jesus breathed (the presence of) Holy Spirit upon the disciples.

What is totally indisputable is that the morning in the upper room is when the power of God the Holy Spirit was released into the church. After His baptism, when Jesus went into the wilderness to be tempted He is described as being **full** of Holy Spirit

(Luke 4:1). When He returned victorious to begin His ministry, it was in the **power** of Holy Spirit (Luke 4:14). He clearly modelled that we need both baptisms for a full and fruitful Christian life.

The story of Peter's shadow in Acts 5:12–16 is a fascinating one. A shadow is not a substance, so it cannot contain healing properties. To quote Bill Johnson again, 'Holy Spirit is in me for my sake but upon me for your sake.' Here we have another example of presence and power combined together, two different aspects of Holy Spirit's work in individual lives. The apostle Peter carried a great **anointing**, the power of Holy Spirit upon him to benefit others. He always carried the presence of Holy Spirit within him, regardless of whether he was in what we might call 'ministry mode' or not.

People knew that Peter carried something special, something powerful, and that, somehow, they could tap into this power by being near him. Therefore, somebody must have been the first to decide to lay a crippled friend somewhere along Peter's typical route to and from the temple for worship. As he passed by, the cripple was healed! Others saw this, or heard about it, and followed suit for the blessing of their friends and family members who were sick or disabled. They each stepped out in faith and received healing miracles.

But they were wrong to attribute these miracles to Peter's shadow, rather than to the anointing he carried, which 'leaked', or overflowed, from him, as he passed by with an open heaven over and around him.

I remember this overflowing of the Spirit being powerfully illustrated by a Roman Catholic monk and nun from a charismatic order, known as the Community of the Beatitudes, at a conference in France a couple of years ago. They took us through the different parts of a Jewish Passover meal. When it came time to serve some wine, they put four empty glasses on a tray and poured wine into them from a decanter. They did not stop when the glasses were full but waited until they were full to overflowing!

There are similar stories of people being impacted by the Spirit overflowing from a person operating under an open heaven. For instance, there are many tales of people being convicted of sin when Smith Wigglesworth passed by them or when he occupied the same railway carriage as them!

Please take encouragement from this story about what Peter carried, because you and I carry it too. Remember what he said to Cornelius?

> As Peter entered the house, Cornelius met him and fell at his feet in reverence. But Peter made him get up. 'Stand up,' he said, 'I am only a man myself.'

> (Acts 10:25–26)

Peter was only a man, but a man who was a born-again believer, baptised in Holy Spirit. Being 'only human' is not, therefore, an acceptable excuse for us not to aspire to emulate Peter, who was himself doing only what Jesus did.

You will have noticed that John 14:12 is mentioned on several occasions in these pages, the promise that we can do what Jesus did and even greater things. If we are born again (presence) and baptised in Holy Spirit (power) and thus have the potential to do even greater things than Jesus, is it not conceivable that this is made possible by an open heaven being over and around us too? Ask yourself, 'Do I really believe, accept and appreciate all of His great and precious promises to me?' (see 2 Peter 1:4)?

As you read this explanation and examples of open heaven do you find yourself challenged as I do? Is this a promise you want to claim, a blessing you want to experience – for the benefit of others? Only you can decide if you are willing to respond to the challenge this makes upon your life, if you have not accepted it already.

As I asked my listeners at the end of my talk on this subject, 'Could this be the time of your breakthrough?'

NOTES

[1] The following thought came into my head one evening during a home-group meeting. I honestly do not know if I was recalling something I had heard before or if I received revelation in that moment: 'The Son of God became the Son of Man in order that the sons (and daughters) of man could become the sons (and daughters) of God.'

POSTSCRIPT

It is not the purpose of this book to go into detail about angels, their existence and their role in Kingdom life, but I would like to leave you with something to consider if, for any reason, you doubt the presence or purpose of angels on assignment on the earth today. I found the following story on Facebook and, if my memory serves me well, it was posted by Bethel Church, Redding, California. A guy named Seth Dahl, a children's leader in that church, had an amazing experience with a group of children there:

> Seth was worshipping with some children and felt himself prompted to ask a 9-year-old girl in the group if she could see angels in the room. He could not actually see any himself. 'Sure, they are over there,' she said, pointing to a corner of the room. 'Why are they here?' Seth asked her. 'I don't know,' she replied. 'Well, please go and ask them,' he responded, and she did this while he kept worshipping with the other children.

She returned, pulled at his shirt and said, 'I know why they are here. For healing.' As she spoke those words, Seth felt an impact in his spirit, so he handed her the microphone and asked her to find out who was sick and send them over to the angels. Seventeen kids responded and, when the girl sent them over to the angels, all seventeen of them were healed!

Chapter 12

---■---

ACTS 29

In my former book, Theophilus, I wrote about all that Jesus began to do and teach ...

(Acts 1:1)

LTHOUGH THE BOOK OF ACTS concludes at the end of chapter 28, the Kingdom story continues and will do so until Jesus returns.

'Acts 29' is both the title and theme of the Saturday seminars and workshops when Cathy and I undertake an Eagles 4031 weekend of ministry with different churches.[1] There is usually a Sunday morning Healing Meeting within which we encourage those who have been with us the day before to minister healing to those who respond to an appeal, either at the end of or during the service. What begins as *our* story, in the introduction, is merged into *their* story as the weekend progresses.

It is revealing to notice how many people start to search their Bibles for this chapter when we announce the title of our specific talk on the subject! We are not trying to catch anyone out, so we remind them very quickly that the book of Acts ends with chapter 28 and add that we do not agree with the theological stance of some that Holy Spirit retired from active ministry then!

He is with us powerfully to this day, encouraging, equipping and empowering us to continue what began with Jesus and is recorded in the 28 chapters of Acts (as well as in the Epistles and Revelation). What has happened since, and will continue until Jesus returns, is what we consider to be the content of 'Acts 29', written in heavenly books.

The Gospels tell us all about the mission of Jesus and the many wonderful things that He did. In the book of Acts, we read about how the apostles and others in the early church carried out His instructions by continuing His mission to bring Heaven to earth. Every one of them was co-missioned to make disciples themselves and to teach them to obey all the commands of Jesus.

That is an ongoing mandate for the Christian church, including you and me. Our adventures contribute to the narrative that is, and will be, Acts 29. It is my story, your story and our story combined to make a Kingdom His-story! This is both challenging and exciting. It is also great fun, so it is no surprise that Romans 14:17 defines the Kingdom of Heaven as 'righteousness, peace and **joy** in the Holy Spirit'.

My story, or our story really because Cathy and I are obviously very much together in this, began from the seed sown through my dramatic healing in May 2008 (as described in Chapter 1). We had some experience of the healing ministry prior to this, from being involved with various church ministry teams, but this was the breakthrough moment opening the way into so much more.

'Freely you have received; freely give' was the key statement (Matthew 10:8) as you will have gathered already. Just as we can comfort others with the comfort with which we have been comforted (2 Corinthians 1:4), so we can bless others with the blessing with which we have been blessed!

We were not sure what was going to happen next, but we did feel led to return to forming, hosting and leading a church home-group at the first opportunity. With the agreement of our church leaders, we began a new group specifically aimed at those interested in exploring with us the healing ministry for today.

We signed up again for ministry team at our church, this being one of the activities that had to be given up when chronic fatigue caused me to cut back on many things prior to the healing experience. In addition, we also applied to join the ministry team for the Detling Summer Celebration, an annual Christian conference held on the Kent County Showground, which had been birthed out of our (then) home church several years previously. Prior to that we had attended regularly as delegates.

I have described elsewhere what happened with the first man we ministered to at Detling. He arrived asking for a chair, because he could not stand for long, and ended up jogging around the site every day for the rest of the week. What an encouragement that was!

I have also mentioned before the influence upon us of the ministry of **Charles** and **Frances Hunter**. 'If Charles and Frances can do it, you can do it, too!' We just 'knew' that God was prompting us to begin a ministry modelled on theirs, in the sense that we would aim to encourage others to get involved in ministering healing rather than having people come out to us alone at the end of a meeting. We have never had any ambition for a platform ministry as 'big names', doing all the 'stuff' ourselves.

Through the Happy Hunters, we were introduced to 'growing out arms and legs' as well as seeing that kind of healing ministry demonstrated by **Mark Marx** (Healing on the Streets) in the same week that we were handed the Hunters' video on the subject.

The following year, at the Detling Summer Celebration, our ministry took further steps forward. I have told you about the two ladies with whiplash injuries. Various other people with skeletal misalignments were also healed. During breaks we often went to the tent set up by our friends, Laurence and Chris, where various folk gathered for coffee, biscuits and a chat. Almost every day found us ministering to someone or other, by their tent, invariably seeing Holy Spirit correcting skeletal misalignments!

This was a time when we also began looking at other healing ministries that were not focused upon the gifting of one person or couple. One of these was the **Healing Rooms** ministry. This is an international ministry, founded by Cal and Michelle Pierce. From a position of senior leadership at Bethel Church, Redding, California, God called them to Spokane, Washington, to 're-dig the wells' of the Healing Rooms ministry founded there by John G. Lake around the time of the First World War. They were obedient to that call and God has blessed them with a ministry that increasingly spreads across the world.

We had the privilege of meeting a couple who co-ordinated this ministry in a little town near the coast of East Sussex. We were invited down to observe a typical evening of ministry. We were early enough to be present for part of the time of preparation, consisting mostly of worship but also of team members encouraging one another with testimonies and prophetic words.

Those coming for ministry gathered in the coffee bar area of the building where worship music was played continuously. When their turn for ministry came, each one was led into another room or area and introduced to the team members who would minister to them, usually a group of three.

One would be 'leader', one in a 'support' role and, if there was a third, he or she was the 'trainee'. They would minister in turn, rotating around the person so that whoever was speaking would be directly in front of them. One would be behind, as a 'catcher' if needed, and the third to one side or the other. They kept in mostly silent communication with each other and changed roles, as they felt led to do so.

We both observed different 'teams', each of them being gracious enough to invite us to share our message if the Lord showed us something. These opportunities to participate meant we were involved in some of the healings ministered, an encouragement to us as well as to the team and their 'customers'!

Mention of **Bill Johnson**, from Bethel Church, Redding, California, cannot be made without acknowledging the positive influence of his teaching upon us, through both books and conferences that we have attended. We have also had the privilege of being in meetings addressed by other ministers/speakers from Bethel (Kris Vallotton, Danny Silk, Joaquin Evans, Chris Gore, Andy Mason and others) as well as reading most of their books.

Books that Bill Johnson has authored with **Randy Clark** (Global Awakening Ministries) have been especially valuable to us. Indeed, whenever I have felt disappointed or discouraged in ministry, for whatever reason, I have found it so therapeutic just to grab one of their books off the shelf, especially *Healing: Unplugged*, to get me back into positive mode again. We also took Bill's advice to 'go where the anointing is' so that we could both learn from and observe other ministries, initially just by volunteering to be 'catchers', in case anyone should fall in the Spirit.

North Kent Community Church (now **Eastgate**) organises many conferences we have attended. The leadership there has been greatly influenced by the Bethel 'culture' and we always felt very much at home in their environment. We became aware of their **Schools of Supernatural Life** and both attended the evening school from 2010 to 2012. This was very helpful and encouraging. We learned a great deal, not least the **Three 'I's**, which we have shamelessly 'pinched' and adapted to our ministry needs. I signed up for two years of day school from 2016 to 2018, which has been time very well spent.

We were also invited to be on the ministry team for some of their conferences, another invaluable aid to our development. Eastgate became our home church in June 2015, where we have served on ministry team as well as on the **Healing Centre** team, which we joined when that ministry began in January 2012. One of its aims is to partner with the National Health Service to bring healing to those who are unable to be helped by current medical knowledge and practice. The church is, as I write, setting in motion a 'Heaven in Healthcare' ministry for medical practitioners across the UK and beyond.

I am an avid reader in my spare time, and not just of Christian literature. I have read as many (Christian) books as I can that refer both to the healing ministry and to those who minister healing.

The series of **God's Generals** books by Roberts Liardon has been of significant benefit. He has also written other historical, biographical books featuring people used by God in the past, from whom we can learn much, not least from their mistakes. Roberts is a revivalist and a powerful speaker whom I have had the privilege of hearing more than once. His most recent God's Generals volume, at the time of writing, features the Hunters and he acknowledges them as probably the first to open the healing ministry to participation by others, as described above.

[In my name] they will place their hands on sick people, and they will get well.

(Mark 16:18, NIV 1984)

This verse is powerfully illustrated in the lives of many whom Roberts writes and speaks about. I often return to these books for both enlightenment and encouragement, having learned to appreciate the power of the testimony. What Jesus has done before He can and will do again. I understand that the root of the Hebrew word translated into English as 'testimony' refers to 'repeating', to 'doing again', underlining the importance of sharing testimonies to encourage one another and to build faith.

I make no apologies for drawing your attention to **John 14:12** again here (come on, you know those precious words of Jesus by heart now!). That great promise is for you and every Christian. You have read a little of our story; what is more important now is your story, your part in Acts 29.

How will you respond to the promises and commands of Jesus? Those whom He calls He equips, but the equipping usually only comes as we respond. Passivity is not an option if we want to see God at work. The statement, 'If Jesus wants to use me He knows my address', is just a cop-out really, isn't it? The ancient Chinese philosopher Lao Tzu said, 'Even a journey of a thousand miles begins with the first step', and that is where our co-operation as the Lord's 'co-labourers' begins.

Anyone can do the possible, but it takes faith and trust in the God of the impossible to participate in the adventure He calls us into. The first part of the journey, for most of us, involves stepping outside our comfort zone. Our comfort zone is any place that we have settled in without the intention of progressing as far as we can beyond it. Every step of faith takes us outside of it into new adventures with God.

There was a lovely picture on Facebook that had two speech bubbles on a blackboard. In the smaller bubble were the words 'Your comfort zone'. In the larger one was written, 'Where the "magic" happens!' We should encourage ourselves to move ourselves from one bubble to the other, which is why the keyword of the Great Commission is 'Go!'

Cathy is, if anything, less naturally disposed than I am to be making a 'cold' approach to strangers, even when the objective is to minister the loving grace of God to them. But, one day, she found herself in the queue at a supermarket checkout behind an elderly man who was clearly having some difficulty in transferring purchases from his basket to the conveyor belt.

She gently enquired if she could help him. He was grateful, explaining that he was suffering from 'frozen shoulder'. Cathy began to assist him, then she found herself saying, 'I'm a Christian and I wonder if you would mind me praying for your shoulder to be healed? I won't do anything weird and people won't know we're doing anything other than having a normal conversation.'

To Cathy's surprise, he agreed, and she briefly addressed the problem in the name of Jesus. As the man was completing his purchase, he started moving his shoulder around and declared that he was healed! They chatted for a few minutes afterwards, during which time he disclosed that he was a Christian and attended a local church, although we are not sure if it is one with an active healing ministry (yet).

This is an example of what can happen to anyone, anytime, anyplace and anywhere if they are open, even if a little reluctantly, to be used of the Lord for His Kingdom purposes. We have dared to call this 'the Martini anointing' but you will have to be of a certain age to remember the TV advertisement this comes from!

So *where* do you go to take your 'First Steps' into healing ministry? If possible, begin in your home church, which should provide a positive, safe, encouraging environment in which to step out for the first time.

But the ultimate purpose should be to take the ministry outside the four walls of the church. Healing and the prophetic are wonderful **evangelistic** 'tools' and, although we are not all called to be evangelists, I believe we are all expected to be evangelistic. Equally, I believe that we are all meant to be prophetic.

A 'Treasure Hunt' is an excellent way of taking the love of God onto the streets. For the benefit of those not familiar with this ministry, or with Kevin Dedmon's book *The Ultimate Treasure Hunt,* I will try to outline briefly the process for you.

People get together in teams of two to four, but no more than six, ideally with members of both genders involved. They each have a pen and a piece of paper or card. The latter is the 'treasure map'. It can be divided into sections with headings like: Location; Name; Appearance; Need; Unusual; and Dates/Numbers. Each person asks Holy Spirit for words of knowledge and writes these down as clues under the most appropriate of those headings.

The person or, more likely, persons that the clues lead you to is/are the treasure you are seeking. Then you go outside to begin looking for them, usually aiming to start at one of the locations you have been given. Scan your 'map' and look for people passing by who match one or more of the clues. When you approach one of them, do not be surprised if their name turns out to be one of those on your 'map'.

A simple introduction would be, 'Excuse me, but we are on a Treasure Hunt and, because you fit in with one [or more] of our "clues", we think that you might be our "treasure". I wonder, do you by any chance ...?' Here you could mention one of the ailments on your 'map'. It can be useful to show the person your 'map' so they can see that you are not making it up.

When it seems best to do so, gently and sensitively explain that you believe that God revealed the clues to you because He wants to bless (the person) today. Then, having received their permission first, proceed as the Lord leads you. It is possible that there is no healing need. If so, trust the Lord for a prophetic word of encouragement to share with the person or find another way, spoken or otherwise, simply to bless them.

A person who is healed is often very receptive to the gospel. Remember, 'the kindness/goodness of God leads to repentance' (see Romans 2:4). But this ministry is exercised as an example of unconditional love, with no strings attached. I have seen men and women of all colours, creeds and religions respond favourably to the love of God expressed to them in these ways. And, often, it is the non-Christians who are most receptive!

Please do not think you are too unworthy to step out in this way. Jesus has made you worthy. He has paid the full price for your entry into His Kingdom as well as to equip you to join His mission to bring Heaven to earth. You do not have to be an apostle, prophet, evangelist, pastor or teacher, with a theological degree, to take an active part in the 'family business' either. The qualifications needed can be found in John 3:16 (whosoever) and in Mark 16:20 (believer). The only essential ability is availability.

Remember that God has already prepared the way (the words of knowledge you have been given are linked to the person they describe). By following your clues to this 'treasure' you are simply tapping into what God is already preparing to do in someone's life. You can always trust Him to equip you for the task He has called you to (see Ephesians 2:10).

You may be like I was and struggle with the idea of a cold approach to a total stranger in the street. I have always been much more comfortable speaking to a church or conference gathering than one to one with a stranger in any environment, whether secular or church. This is one of the main reasons that I decided to sign up for ESSL. Day school students go into Gravesend every Friday to minister on the streets, anything from prophetic words (from photographs chosen by passers-by from those on display) through free hugs to treasure hunting. This was a 'chicken line' I just knew God wanted me to cross.

My first ESSL treasure hunt began with a gathering together of the team in a town centre coffee bar to write out our treasure maps. I shared a table with two other students, a second-year to keep an eye on us and another first-year (from France). As we were writing down our clues, we each discovered that fine gold dust had appeared on our hands.[2] In my case, it was covering both my palms and my fingers. I took this to be an answer to my prayer for the Lord to encourage me that day and, when my turn came to approach someone, I did it without a quibble. I got to pray with the man concerned (he had a walking stick with him but was sitting down). Because his English was very limited, it was difficult to ascertain if he received a measure of healing or not. To be honest, and perhaps to my shame, I was more excited about my own breakthrough!

For my second treasure hunt, three weeks later, I was paired with a fellow first-year student (from Kenya this time). As we were writing down our clues, I found gold dust on my hands again. This time it was on my fingers only, and I was disappointed, feeling short-changed. Immediately, I sensed God saying to me, 'No, it's OK, you just don't need as much encouragement this time.'

He was right (no surprise!). *Jeanette* and I took it in turns to approach five or six people on the streets, from our clues, neither of us having any problem making these approaches. We 'prayed' for most of the people and blessed the others. The last one, a lady who lined up with four of Jeanette's clues, was particularly touched by the love of God and her eyes filled with tears of gratitude.

God is so good, and this ministry is so rewarding. Holy Spirit does what He does best – as you co-operate with Him (without striving). It's fun! It's God's Kingdom – on earth as it is in Heaven! Go for it!

NOTES

[1] You can obtain further information and/or contact details through our website, www.eagles4031.org.uk, if you would be interested in discussing the possibility of us coming to your church for a weekend or to engage with a group of interested Christians in some other (healing ministry) context.

[2] I realise that talking about manifestations of gold dust, feathers, jewels, etc., will be controversial in some circles. I have witnessed these things, the appearance of gold dust being very common at Eastgate, although it had never appeared on my body before. If something like this becomes visible where there was no sign of it just beforehand, and it spreads before your eyes, you know it must be a creative sign of the presence of God. We don't need to read any more into it than that. And, of course, *I know* what it has been my privilege to see and experience, whether other people choose to believe me or not.

Chapter 13

HIS PRESENCE

And surely I am with you always, to the very end of the age.

(Matthew 28:20)

WHAT A COMFORT AND A BLESSING it is to know that the Lord is with us always, no matter who we are, where we go or what we are doing. We can rejoice and be at peace with the assurance that comes with such knowledge. But He has not chosen to be with us always solely for our own sakes, just for our own personal edification. He is also present with us for the benefit of *others* and equips us for everything He has prepared for us to do to bless them.

When we are born again, or born from above, by the intervention of Holy Spirit (John 3:3), we can be assured of His presence with us for the rest of our lives here on earth, and forever when we go 'home' to Heaven. This is one thing that will never be taken from us, but Jesus promised us even more (John 14:16–20): what is commonly termed as 'the baptism of the Holy Spirit'.

> [John the Baptist said] I baptise you with water for repentance. But after me comes one who is more powerful than I, whose sandals I am not worthy to carry. He will baptise you with the Holy Spirit and fire.
>
> (Matthew 3:11)

After we are born again, we can be baptised both in water and in Holy Spirit: the essential combination of Presence and Power for a fruitful Christian life. Both these experiences are, or can be, common to all Christians, but it is good for us to be reminded that they were denied to John the Baptist himself.

When Jesus came to be baptised by him in the Jordan, John responded by saying that he was the one who needed to be baptised (by Jesus). By this I believe he meant with the baptism in Holy Spirit. It is amazing to read Jesus' commendation of John in Matthew 11 and yet discover that the person who is least in the Kingdom of Heaven is deemed to be greater than him!

Surely this can only mean because of the privilege we have, under the new covenant, to be baptised in Holy Spirit? Although John features in the Gospels he was, in fact, the last of the Old Covenant prophets and was therefore limited by the constraints of that covenant. All the blessings of the superior New Covenant were not available to him as they are for each of us.

Of course, Jesus, as the Son of Man, went through baptism in water (for the sake of righteousness) and baptism in Holy Spirit, Who descended upon Him in the form of a dove – and remained (Presence). On seeing this happen, John understood it to be the fulfilment of God's commissioning word to him. From that moment on, John knew that his mission had been completed, that he could withdraw from the scene and let Jesus take centre stage. I believe this to be the true meaning of John 3:30, and not the way it is often interpreted and then applied to each one of us. I'll leave you to ponder that.

Now if Jesus, as the Son of Man, needed the baptism of Holy Spirit for the empowerment of His human life and ministry, how much more do you and I! I have already indicated that Jesus, never ceasing to be the Son of God, the second Person of the Holy Trinity, voluntarily laid aside His majesty, the glories of His divinity, to minister here on earth as a human being fully surrendered to the will of the Father and the empowering presence of Holy Spirit. It is for this reason alone that we can aspire to do the things that He did, and even greater things (John 14:12 again!).

In Luke 4 we find out what happened to Jesus after His double baptism. He returned from the Jordan '**full** of the Holy Spirit' and was led by the Spirit into the desert. There He experienced a major challenge to His ministry and calling (*identity*) from the devil himself. Jesus emerged victorious from this confrontation and returned to Galilee 'in the **power** of the [Holy] Spirit'. That is the explosive combination of Presence and Power again!

Then we discover that He went into the synagogue at Nazareth and read to the congregation from the powerful opening verses of Isaiah 61. He put down the scroll and astonished His listeners by declaring that He was the fulfilment of those verses. 'The Spirit of the Lord is upon me …' He stated and, by so doing, He confirmed what He had both experienced and was experiencing; the Dove having rested upon Him and remained (Presence).

In Acts 1:5 and 8 Jesus tells His followers that they would also be baptised in Holy Spirit (fullness) and that they would therefore receive power for their ministry as His witnesses to the world.

This is true for each one of us also because He told
them to:

> Go and make disciples of all nations, baptising them in the
> name of the Father and of the Son and of the Holy Spirit,
> and teaching them to obey everything I have commanded
> you. And surely I am with you always, to the very end of
> the age.

(Matthew 28:19–20)

There, at the end, we have again the promise of His presence. And
the Great Commission could not be accomplished without Divine
Power. We have the privilege to be carriers of the presence of
God wherever we go, coupled with the encouragement to 'leak' (or
'overflow'). The baptism of Holy Spirit is not a one-off experience
but is necessarily repeatable.

An example of this is found in Acts 4:31. At least some of those
present at that time must have been around on the Day of Pentecost
(Acts 2), when Peter 'leaked' the first Christian sermon. After that,
while Peter and John were before the Sanhedrin (Acts 4:8) Peter is
described as 'filled' with Holy Spirit, so he was obviously refilled
on more than one occasion!

The true state of being filled is demonstrated, not by being
filled to the brim, but by being filled to the point of overflowing.
When I spoke on this matter at a conference in France in May
2016, the translator rendered the English word 'leaking', which I
used, as the French equivalent of the word 'overflowing'! I will say
more about that later.

Earlier, in the same conference, we were treated to a Shabbat
(Sabbath) meal, complete with teaching about the significance of
the different elements of the meal and what it means to the participants who experience it. As already mentioned, when the wine

was to be served four glasses were provided on a tray. A jug was used to decant the wine into the glasses and Frère Jean-Marie, who was performing this task, did not stop when the first glass was full. Instead he continued to pour until the wine overflowed from it onto the tray. What an amazing illustration of being filled with the presence of Holy Spirit!

I do not want to go into overkill, but I think it is so important to emphasise how vital it is to be baptised in, and continuously refilled with, Holy Spirit, and how this is synonymous with being a carrier of the Presence (of God). Apart from Him we can do nothing of (Kingdom) value and significance! Let me just draw your attention to two passages in Acts, 8:14–7 and 19:6, that make the point most forcibly.

The first instance is where Peter and John went down to Samaria after the apostles in Jerusalem had heard what had happened there through the ministry of Philip. They rejoiced over the new converts, but they noticed immediately that they had not been baptised in Holy Spirit and so the apostles set about remedying that omission. The other passage referred to above illustrates the same thing when Paul came upon some new converts in Ephesus.

As carriers of the Presence, that is, those who are baptised in Holy Spirit, we are warned not to '**quench**' the Spirit (1 Thessalonians 5:19) and not to '**grieve**' Him (Ephesians 4:30). The implication of these words is that He is the most sensitive Person of the Trinity, albeit that He is as strong and as powerful as the Father and the Son.

Bill Johnson has a wonderful teaching on how to ensure that the Dove remains upon us and is not given cause to fly away. He says that we should do everything with the Dove in mind. We should always be conscious of His presence and think, live and act accordingly. By so doing we will find that our lives are more clearly marked both by the 'fruit of the Spirit' (Galatians 5:22–23) and by the 'gifts of the Spirit' (e.g. Hebrews 2:4).

If we conduct ourselves in submission to, and with full awareness of, the presence of Holy Spirit in us, we will 'leak', or 'overflow', His characteristics in our interaction with others. That is the fruit of the Spirit, nine examples of which are given in the passage in Galatians 5.

Not only that but also, when action is called for, we will be available to minister His goodness and grace through any gift of the Spirit relevant to the prevailing circumstances. He distributes them as He wills for the common good (1 Corinthians 12:7, 11), that is, for the benefit of others.

Going back to the conference in France I referred to earlier, the theme of the weekend was '*Faire tomber les murs*' in French or, in English, 'Breaking down the walls'. In my talk, I made the point that, in worldly terms, breaking down walls would conjure up images of the very large machinery and tools employed in the modern demolition business. We even find an example of demolishing walls in the Bible (Joshua 6), although the only tools the people used there, in addition to their marching feet, were trumpets!

I went on to say that the means employed under the New Covenant would perhaps be a little different and suggested that, now, we could find ourselves breaking down walls by being carriers of the presence of God.

In this context, I referred the delegates to 'walls' that we erect for self-protection. Non-Christians could do this to deflect the message of the gospel away from them. Christians can erect 'walls' too, or they continue to hide behind 'walls' that were part of their life experience before conversion, often unknowingly. We even have 'walls' in the form of denominational barriers or other means of division that we create within the church universal.

Some of us are bound by events or habits from the past that might be better described as 'chains' rather than walls. Neither walls nor chains are healthy, and we need the power (in the Presence) of God to deal with them. There were a couple of examples of the latter on my visit to India in October 2015.

Before leaving the UK, a friend from Eastgate offered to pray for me. He also ended up prophesying that, during the trip, I would find myself 'breaking chains' in Jesus' name. I had no idea what that would mean in practice but shared it with Phil, who I made the journey with, during our long flight to Mumbai.

One of our first engagements was a conference for a group of pastors from a rural area who travelled to where we were staying because they came from a region Westerners were advised not to travel to and where there remained a degree of hostility towards both Christians and the gospel.

As Phil and I were praying before the first session, I shared with him that the word 'freedom' was being impressed strongly upon me and I reminded him also about the prophecy I had received back home. He was happy to 'go for it' however the Lord led us.

As the meeting progressed I became aware that at least some of the pastors could be still in 'bondage' to old traditions that would probably serve to impair the effectiveness of their ministries in modern times. I shared this with them and invited those with whom the concept resonated to stand in a circle around the room with their arms outstretched in front of them. It was very interesting to note that they all chose to join in.

Holding their hands a few inches apart, so that it looked as though they were each encumbered by invisible handcuffs (or manacles/chains), I led them in a prayer. After pausing for a few moments to allow them to articulate individually before the Lord what each one felt their personal bondages to be, I invited them to violently pull their hands further apart as though breaking the invisible 'chains' (or handcuffs) that held them. These guys do not give too much away by their facial expressions or body language, but subsequent feedback from the conference organisers indicated that many had been positively impacted by this prophetic act.

Towards the end of the trip we found ourselves ministering in a comparatively new church in a slum area of the main city of the region we went to. There were many ladies present and I had learned that, even in the church, it was still not unusual for women to be treated as second-class citizens. This is a cultural tradition that is still a problem for many and, of course, is contrary to the gospel message of equality between the sexes.

Phil agreed, when I had shared the idea with him, that it would be right to break these cultural chains. He had visited the city many times before and knew that the pastor (actually Ravi, mentioned in an earlier chapter) would not be averse to us doing this. I led the women in the same prophetic act as I had the men earlier in the week but, obviously, with a different prayer. When the 'chains' were broken most, if not all, of the women were moved to tears as they experienced breakthrough into new freedom in Christ.

There are places where the presence of God seems to be experienced more tangibly than in others. This is usually equated with an 'open heaven' (see Chapter 11) over that location. The Celtic Christians would refer to it as a 'thin place'. The meaning of both terms is that any barrier between Heaven and earth would be either absent or virtually non-existent there (i.e. open heaven). One example of this, in the UK, is Ffald y Brenin in Wales, a place Cathy and I had the privilege of visiting in 2016.

Our friend, Paul Bennison, is convinced that there is an open heaven over the city of Cali in Colombia, where he ministers regularly. Given the amazing miracles that have happened there over the past 20 years, during his visits, I am certainly not going to contest that assertion!

We often encounter the tangible presence of God in church meetings during especially powerful times of worship. He is present everywhere all the time but there is no doubt that His presence is more obvious on some occasions than on others. Consequently, we always recommend times of worship (and testimonies) before church meetings, not least when healing ministry is expected to be part of the proceedings.

The word for 'glory' in the Bible, a manifestation of the presence of God, has 'heavy' or 'weight' at the root of its original meaning and, if you have ever experienced the tangible presence of God, either alone or in a meeting, you will understand why that makes such good sense.

To further illustrate the weighty, tangible presence of God and His impact upon people, I wonder if you have heard about the experience of people who attended prayer meetings with Smith Wigglesworth? Stories are told of people leaving the room one by one because they could not remain in the increasing heaviness of Holy Presence in the place, until only Wigglesworth was left. Here was a man who had grown used to being in the powerful presence of God and did not feel the need to flee, in fear of his life, as others seemed to!

It is not difficult to equate 'sickness' and 'demonic oppression' with 'walls' or 'chains' and, as carriers of the Presence, we are in the family business with Holy Spirit to destroy the works of the devil (1 John 3:8). Sometimes it is necessary to go about this forcefully, or aggressively, using the authority we have in Christ, but that is not always so. Hence, we find Jesus equating us with 'salt' and 'light' in Matthew 5:13–14, 16.

We know that, in the time of Jesus' earthly ministry, salt was used to preserve meat. The church acts as a preservative today, to some degree, as we carry the presence of God wherever we go in this world. But I believe that, in this context, Jesus was focusing more on the equally valuable function of salt to add, or bring out, flavour.

Salt not only adds its own flavour, but it enhances, or draws out, existing flavours. As Christians, we are to add flavour to the life of the communities in which we live, work and minister. We need to have more faith and confidence in the impact that the presence of Holy Spirit, both in us and overflowing from us, will have on those around us, especially non-Christians.

> Do you show contempt for the riches of his kindness, for-
> bearance and patience, not realising that God's kindness is
> intended to lead you to repentance?
>
> (Romans 2:4)

It is God's kindness, or goodness, perhaps most clearly demon-strated through healing, that is much more likely to lead someone to repentance than a 'hell-fire' sermon that seeks to frighten them into the Kingdom!

To be truly effective evangelistically, we must genuinely value people *before* they have come to faith, just as Jesus did. Each one of us, whether we know and acknowledge Him or not, is made in the image of God. We read in the Gospels how sinners were drawn to Jesus, who truly represented the Father, in a way that they never were to the religious establishment figures of the day. I am inclined to suggest that nothing much has changed in that regard!

So, let us encourage one another to be not only a preservative in our communities but also to add and to enhance Kingdom flavours as we consciously carry His presence wherever we may go.

His presence is also described as 'Light'. Jesus is truly the Light of the world, but He is also the One who describes us with the same words. He expects us to let this Light shine before others, because we have a part to play in drawing them into the Kingdom.

As they see our good deeds, ministering healing for example, they
will give glory to our Father in Heaven, the One who enables the
works to be accomplished. Isaiah prophesied concerning both Jesus
and us in this context:

> Arise, shine, for your light has come, and the glory of
> the LORD rises upon you. See, darkness covers the earth
> and thick darkness is over the peoples, but the LORD rises
> upon you and his glory appears over you. Nations will
> come to your light, and kings to the brightness of your
> dawn.
>
> (Isaiah 60:1–3)

Light shines most brightly in the darkness. We need not be afraid
of going where 'darkness' is, or of being adversely affected by it
when we do. Why should we be if we are fully aware of the Light
we carry and its total superiority over darkness? The inferior will
always be subject to the superior.

> The one who is in you is greater than the one who is in
> the world.
>
> (1 John 4:4b)

Light dispels darkness – switch on a light in a dark room and the
darkness disappears. Light attracts – people are attracted to a city
on a hill. Light also exposes that which is hidden (in 'darkness').
Heavenly Light uncovers the works of the enemy, such as deception.
And we are carriers of that Light because we are carriers of His
presence.

We are the 'salt of the earth' and the 'light of the world' by the
grace of God and His presence within us and upon us. We carry
that presence into every situation we encounter. We just need to
be aware of what we carry and be open to what God is prepared

to do in the lives of those who are drawn to His presence in us and 'leaking', or overflowing, from us.

Looking back into the Old Testament, we find that Moses was one who placed great store by the presence of God. His was an unusually intimate relationship with God for those times:

> Whenever the people saw the pillar of cloud standing at the entrance to the tent, they all stood and worshipped, each at the entrance to their tent. The LORD would speak to Moses face to face, as one speaks to a friend.
>
> (Exodus 33:10)

He was also very aware of the need for the people to know the presence of God, insofar as it was possible under the Old Covenant. Moses even told God that he was not prepared to lead the Israelites into the Promised Land without the assurance of God's presence going with them. Even the promise of an angelic guide was not sufficient for him. His relationship with God was such that he had the courage to challenge what God said to Him. This only served to deepen further the relationship between them!

> The LORD replied, 'My Presence will go with you, and I will give you rest.' Then Moses said to him, 'If your Presence does not go with us, do not send us up from here. How will anyone know that you are pleased with me and with your people unless you go with us? What else will distinguish me and your people from all the other people on the face of the earth?'
>
> (Exodus 33:14–16)

David was another Old Testament character who valued the presence of God. He proposed a programme of day and night worship and the tangible presence of God was evident when the temple, built eventually by Solomon, was consecrated:

> When Solomon finished praying, fire came down from heaven and consumed the burnt offering and the sacrifices, and the glory of the LORD filled the temple. The priests could not enter the temple of the LORD because the glory of the LORD filled it. When all the Israelites saw the fire coming down and the glory of the LORD above the temple, they knelt on the pavement with their faces to the ground, and they worshipped and gave thanks to the LORD, saying, 'He is good; his love endures for ever.'
>
> (2 Chronicles 7:1–3)

In various ways, God's tangible presence may still be experienced today. This is especially true in worship but also happens during times of ministry of other kinds, including healing.

When ministering healing it is important to function from a place of rest, or peace. The rest/peace is *within* us and is in no way dependent upon what may be happening around us. Nothing should be allowed to distract us from our awareness of the presence of God at such times. Peace undergirds confidence, and even desperation leads us to Him when we live from that place of rest.

Let me finish this chapter by sharing a lovely testimony from *Rod*, a pastor who was going on holiday and was waiting in a UK airport, with his wife, for his flight to be called. Rod is the sort of person who is always open to what Holy Spirit might be doing and has an insatiable desire to be involved in what the Lord wants to accomplish at any given moment.

However, Rod had promised his wife that he would be on his 'best behaviour' for their holiday and would just relax and not go looking for encounter opportunities! Sitting together over a cup of coffee, while they were waiting for the boarding call, he got bored. So, he decided to just 'leak' Holy Spirit and see what happened.

It was not long before someone who had been either sitting or standing some 20–30 metres away from Rod, on the other side of the departure area, wandered across and said something like this to him: 'I don't understand why, but I feel drawn to come over and speak to you. What is going on here, please?' The person turned out to be a Christian, and a special time of sharing and ministry took place before it was time to catch the flight!

Be encouraged, as a carrier of the Presence, to gently, lovingly, graciously, compassionately and gloriously break down the 'walls' of opposition to the Kingdom, whatever form they may take, and set free those who are bound in 'chains'. This is your (new) birthright.

Chapter 14

STEPPING OUT
(A CASE STUDY)

One day Peter and John were going up to the temple at the time of prayer ...

(Acts 3:1–26)

THE STORY OF THE ENCOUNTER THAT Peter and John had with the crippled man at the Beautiful Gate of the temple in Jerusalem provides a wonderful illustration for us of how to minister to the sick. It underlines the guidelines I have tried to provide in these pages and we can learn much by taking note of what happened on that day. Without wishing to get into formulae, this is almost a perfect template for ministering to the sick outside the four walls of a church building.

Although this encounter did not happen within the temple (church building) itself, we find that Peter and John were on their way to the temple for what was probably one of the fixed times for prayer observed in Judaism. Possibly they went at other times of the day as well; certainly we read back in Acts chapter 2 that the new believers met together within the temple courts every day. So, although they were going to the temple at one of the daily prayer times, it may well be that it was for a meeting with those of the growing number of new Christian believers who were also able to attend.

There is no indication that they were on a 'treasure hunt' *en route* (see Acts 9:10–12), but I think they were always open to approach anyone that Holy Spirit might choose to 'highlight' to them. We are not told this, but they may even have 'seen' the beggar through a word of knowledge while praying together before they set out. No doubt they were always alert to every possibility wherever they went (see 1 Peter 3:15), motivated by the practice that Heidi Baker advocates of 'stopping for the one'.

What we can be pretty certain about is that, on this particular occasion, they were to approach this particular man. We are given to understand that he had been born a cripple and that he was taken to the temple courts every day to beg from the worshippers. We are not given any indication of his age, but it seems fair to say that he would have been at his post on many other occasions when Peter and John walked to the temple, almost certainly even when Jesus made the same journey, but *this* was to be his time.

The beggar opened the conversation by asking the apostles for money, so Peter and John didn't have to make the 'Excuse me ...' approach themselves on this occasion. It may be that the circumstances working out like this served as confirmation that Holy Spirit was choosing to be active on this particular day (where He had not on all of the other days in the past when they had passed by the beggar). Sometimes, with healing, it is all about timing, and that is usually in God's hands.

I say 'usually' because I am reminded of a famous (or infamous, depending upon your point of view) statement that

Smith Wigglesworth made: 'If the Holy Spirit does not move, then I move the Holy Spirit.' I personally believe that all Wigglesworth meant by this was that he had sufficient faith and confidence in God that, if he stepped out in faith, Holy Spirit would back him up. After all, this is not an unreasonable stance if, like him, you have settled in your heart that it is always God's will to heal. Then it could even be argued that 'usually' does not come into the equation anyway!

Peter and John looked straight at the beggar. We are not told why they did this, but perhaps there is a clue in Acts 14:9, describing Paul's experience in Lystra. When Paul looked directly at a lame man there, he 'saw' that he had faith to be healed. That encounter proceeded very much like this one.

Peter and John instructed the beggar to look at them. This could be how they 'saw' that this man had faith to be healed, but it is unlikely because we are told that he responded positively only because he expected to receive some money. On the other hand, this may be how they 'knew' that Holy Spirit was 'on' that man. In other words, they could have experienced a 'knowing' that Holy Spirit was present to heal (Luke 5:17).

Peter then ministered healing to the man, in the name of Jesus, with full confidence and authority. This was not done in hope or in (hopeful) faith, but with confident expectation. By this time, Peter had clearly reached the stage where he expected God to act in response to his faith (i.e. total trust in Him to be true to His promises).

A further illustration of Peter's total conviction is that, apparently before any sign of healing was obvious, he stretched out his hand to help the beggar to his feet. That really is a step of faith and not something that would be recommended by most teachers when talking about and/or demonstrating the healing ministry! What is most likely, I think, is that Peter received a 'gift of faith' (see 1 Corinthians 12:9) for that moment. Most teachers would agree that, when that happens, it is safe to override the suggested guidelines that we are being asked to follow in normal circumstances.

We are not told that Peter dragged him up from his supine position, so I think it probable that the beggar had 'caught' something of Peter's faith (even if he did not understand what was happening) and co-operated willingly. In that moment, his feet and ankles instantly became strong, he jumped to his feet, and began to walk.[1] This, again, is exactly the same experience as the man in Lystra enjoyed (Acts 14:10).

The ex-beggar proceeded to join with Peter and John in their walk to the temple, now 'walking and jumping'! No doubt the three men entered into some sort of conversation on the way and it was what Peter and John had to say that convinced the man that God had healed him. However it happened, he began praising God, which indicates that the man attributed his healing to God rather than to His human emissaries.

Many people saw him walking, jumping and praising, and recognised him as the beggar from the Beautiful Gate. This grabbed their attention, so Peter seized the opportunity to give a short evangelistic address, during which he did not pull any punches. He was out to win converts, not friends! First of all, though, he gave the glory to God for this miracle.

He made it clear that the healing had nothing to do with any power or godliness of Peter and John themselves. Of course, the power was released through them and so they were God's *co*-workers in the performance of this miracle. Also, their godliness was involved, too. But, just as we do not trust in a righteousness of our own but in that which is imparted to us by Jesus, so anything approaching godlikeness in us comes from Him and is ours by grace. It was not their power or godliness that enabled the miracle, but there would have been no miracle without their willing and faithful *co*-operation in the purposes of God. The humility they expressed was not false humility.

Immediately, Peter directed attention away from John and himself to Jesus. It was in His name and for a revelation of His glory that the healing occurred. It was in Jesus' name[2] and through the faith that comes through Him (this could be either saving faith [Ephesians 2:8–9] or the gift of faith [see above]) that this 'complete healing' came.

So, Peter reminds his hearers of what had happened to Jesus of Nazareth in Jerusalem only a short while before. He makes it clear that both that mockery of a trial and the subsequent crucifixion were, to some extent, their responsibility. But then he expressed compassion by acknowledging that they had acted in ignorance, actually complying with the purposes of God for salvation by endorsing what happened to Jesus. He also points out that the death and resurrection of Jesus was what had been foretold by the prophets.

Peter concludes by issuing a call to repentance, just as he did at Pentecost in the first Christian sermon. We are not told what the immediate response of the people was, because the religious authority figures and the temple guard came and interrupted proceedings by arresting Peter and John (in Acts 4). But later, in verse 4, we read that 'many who heard the message believed, and the number of men grew to about five thousand' (NIV 1984).

There were three thousand added to their number at Pentecost and, while we don't know how many came to faith between these two incidents, the number must have been substantial to get to a total of five thousand, and that was just the men!

This is a perfect illustration of my point about healing being a very effective 'tool' for evangelism and the kindness (or goodness) of God leading people to repentance (Romans 2:4).

I have called this chapter a 'Case Study' because it is a biblical example of a healing miracle leading to many people coming to Christ, not just the one who was healed – although that would be a substantial reward in itself.

Peter and John were open to the possibility of Holy Spirit leading them to someone in order that, by the grace and through the gifts of God, they could be used to facilitate an encounter between God and a needy individual. They were obedient to His promptings and stepped out in faith when the opportunity was presented to them. They ministered in the powerful name of Jesus, and by faith in Him, resulting in the beggar being miraculously healed.

When the now former beggar became aware of how his healing had come about, he responded by praising God and, by implication at least, giving his life to Jesus. Peter took the opportunity of the stir that was caused by the man walking, jumping and praising God, to speak evangelistically to all within earshot. As a result, a large number of people also came to Christ.

My prayer is that this will be an encouragement to you and me to step out in faith, on a regular basis, and trust God to back us up, believing that it is His will to heal and also to save (2 Peter 3:9). Remember, it is our job to step out, and it is His job to do what only He can (e.g. to heal). Our faith is expressed in the 'Excuse me' moment.

Are **you** ready to step out, whether or not that means these will be your *first steps into healing as part of your normal, everyday Christian life?*

'God is not looking for experts but for His children.'

'He wants our agreement, our willingness, not our expertise.'

(Joaquin Evans – Bethel, Austin, Texas)

NOTES

[1] On a similar note, during our trip to Colombia late in 2017, Cathy had the privilege of ministering (in a church building) to a young lady who was in considerable pain, due to having been shot in the knee. After a few words of prayer ministry, translated from English into Spanish, she pronounced herself pain free and began jumping up and down with joy, praising God!

[2] 'What a powerful name it is' is part of the lyric of a worship song that focuses on the name of Jesus. *Janine*, a first-year student at ESSL, shared a testimony that wonderfully illustrates this truth.

She was walking in a seaside town where there are a number of homeless people. She felt Holy Spirit drawing her to a particular guy who was sitting on a suitcase and holding his shoulder. She sensed the Lord asking her to give him some money for a hot meal and to pray for his shoulder, so she stepped over her 'chicken line' to approach him. She handed him some money and he thanked her and said this was just what he needed to buy a hot meal.

Feeling encouraged by that, she asked him if he was in pain and he indicated his shoulder, explaining that there had been an altercation the previous night with a couple of blokes who had tried to steal his suitcase and he believed his shoulder was dislocated. He agreed to her request to pray for him.

She got no further than 'Jesus ...', when he suddenly jumped back and shouted out, 'What the [blankety-blank] did you just do to me?!' Surprised, she explained that she had begun to pray but only got to speak that one word before he reacted. He said that someone had suddenly manipulated his shoulder back into place!

Relieved, she told him that the name of Jesus is very powerful and was more than enough to facilitate his healing!

Chapter 15

■

HOW TO HEAL THE SICK?

Heal the sick who are there and tell them, 'The kingdom of God is near you.'

(Luke 10:9, NIV 1984)

NO MATTER HOW WELL-MEANING THEIR authors may be, I am always very wary of those Christian books that offer us 'the [so many] keys to [whatever]' or instruct us exactly how we should do this, that or the other. So, you will understand my reluctance to include in this book a 'How to …' chapter about Christian healing!

We must be so careful not to adopt a formulaic approach, based either on what we have just read or on what happened last time in a similar situation. Instead we should always, always remain open to the leading of Holy Spirit. As we read the Gospel accounts of the healing of the blind or the leprous, we find that Jesus was not restricted to one 'method' of healing for each affliction.

You will recall that, as the Son of Man, He said this about His ministry works:

> Very truly I tell you, the Son can do nothing by himself; he can do only what he sees his Father doing, because whatever the Father does the Son also does.

> (John 5:19)

Lest we should assume that Father God got Holy Spirit to play a video of what He had in mind in Jesus' head before He stepped out, may I suggest that the word 'sees' in this verse might be better understood as 'perceived'. Jesus was not a pre-programmed robot and that is not what He is modelling for us.

We do well to remember that God is sovereign which, in simple terms, means that He can do whatever He likes, whenever He likes and however He likes to do it. He alone is the Healer and we are totally dependent upon Him for effective ministry. Nevertheless, observation and experience can provide us with some useful guidelines, provided we never let them take precedence over how Holy Spirit seeks to lead us in every individual situation.

SETTLE THE ISSUE

It really is essential, before we start, to get it straight in our minds about the will of God to heal today. The Lord's Prayer contains the lines, 'Your kingdom come, your will be done on earth as it is in heaven.' There is no sickness in Heaven and our fundamental mission/ministry is to bring the Kingdom of Heaven to earth by facilitating heavenly encounters.

Healing is an expression of the unconditional love of God for all His children. It is an important aspect of **salvation**, translated from the Greek word *sozo* meaning forgiveness plus healing and deliverance. Our theology of healing should be based on the Word of God and not upon our previous experience, especially if that falls short of what the Bible clearly states.

PRESENCE

Learning to recognise and to depend upon the presence of God is of paramount importance. When ministering, faith will attract Him, and answers from Him, but presumption will not. Presumption is not genuine faith; it can just give the impression that it might be. It is our confidence in His presence, in who He is and all that He is, that moves Him to respond to the needs we bring before Him. One helpful definition of faith is, 'my connection with God'.

TWO BY TWO

When Jesus sent out the Twelve and the Seventy (or Seventy-two), they travelled around in pairs (see Luke 10:1). This provides companionship, mutual encouragement and the opportunity for a mixture of gifts, not just 'your own', to be utilised.

My advice is to minister healing in pairs whenever possible, ideally one male and one female. Unless you are in a group environment, and there really is no alternative, it is better for a male not to minister alone to a female and vice versa. Sadly, it is possible for over-dependency, or worse, to be created out of any ministry connection. Operating in pairs will reduce the risk of this happening.

The worst-case scenario for a ministry combination involving a lone male to/from a lone female is that it can escalate into a sexual relationship. The devil will do everything possible to discredit the healing ministry and the best form of defence is to never give him any opportunity. A husband and wife team are a great pairing, especially if they are compatible in ministry situations. Not all married couples are, but that would be the exception rather than the norm.

If you know each other's strengths and weaknesses, then it is much easier to ensure that the 'right' person is leading the ministry time at any given stage. With Cathy and me, she will usually take the lead with emotional healing and I will do so with physical healing or deliverance. This is certainly not a hard and fast *modus operandi* as we are always ready to communicate so that we can change 'roles' as and when it seems right to do so.

When ministering at the Healing Centre, usually with a different partner every time, I always prefer it if the female partner takes the 'lead' when we introduce ourselves to a female 'client', and vice versa. It is important for the 'client' to feel relaxed as quickly as possible and this is just one way of enabling that to happen. The baton can be passed back and forth, as is deemed necessary, as the ministry time progresses.

When ministering on the streets in some capacity, then to do so in pairs is very important as it is a non-threatening approach to whomever the Lord has highlighted to you. The female partner taking the lead in the 'Excuse me' stage, if a woman is highlighted, is essential here, in my opinion. More than two people together can be threatening to some.

DON'T BE BLINKERED!

Praying with our eyes shut is a habit most, if not all, of us have acquired over the years. There is nothing wrong with that, but ministering healing is not the same as what we might call 'ordinary' praying. May I encourage you always to minister with your eyes open. Not only does this enable you to see how the person is reacting (or manifesting), but also you can have eye contact with your partner, which aids communication between you, at least some of which will be unspoken, if you work well together.

My suggestion would be for one of you to stand[1] in front of the person being ministered to, and the other either to one side or behind them. This will not only aid communication between you but, if the person is about to fall under the power of Holy Spirit, you will almost certainly anticipate it, with your eyes open. It is easier to catch them if two are ministering together, with the one to the side or behind them being alert to the possibility of a 'fall'.

In the unlikely event of any problem arising it means that, with two ministering together with their eyes open, there will always be another witness to what happened during the ministry time. Let's be both cautious and sensible when we minister, recognising that there are some 'rogue' people about with an agenda to discredit the church!

FAITH ACTIVATION

Faith is an important factor in the healing ministry and sometimes, but certainly not always, faith on the part of the person being ministered to may be called for:

> 'Stretch out your hand' [said Jesus]. So he stretched it out and it was completely restored, just as sound as the other.
>
> (Matthew 12:13)

If the man had not stretched out his hand, then I do not believe he would have been (instantly) healed. His co-operation is an example of faith in action.

We find the same sort of situation with the blind man whom Jesus sent to wash his eyes:

'Go,' he told him, 'wash in the Pool of Siloam.' ... So, the
man went and washed, and came home seeing.

(John 9:7)

I think it is obvious it would not have happened like that if the
blind man had failed to combine faith with obedience. After all, it
was not the water that healed him!

Another example of 'faith in action' is found in the account of
the healing of the ten lepers:

When [Jesus] saw them, he said, 'Go, show yourselves to
the priests.' And as they went, they were cleansed.

(Luke 17:14)

There was no healing until sometime during their walk towards
the place where the priests were.

The classic example is the healing of Naaman, the mighty
Syrian general, as recorded in 2 Kings 5:1–15. He had to be
persuaded to do something very mundane, something that he felt
was beneath him, in order to obtain his healing. He needed to
demonstrate, with humility, that he believed the prophet's words.
You may recall that this was the scenario that God brought to
my mind when I was directed to touch the television screen
for Him to heal me from ME. Putting even a little mustard seed faith
into action was as valuable for me as it was for General Naaman!

Don't be surprised, therefore, if you are prompted by Holy
Spirit to ask someone to do something while you are ministering to him or her. Sometimes this may be nothing more than
requesting them to move the damaged part of their body, after
you have 'prayed' for it, to test out the healing. If they can now
do what they could not do before, either at all or not without

experiencing pain, you have an excellent progress report. You could be prompted to do this even if there has been no obvious sign of any healing/improvement up to that point. Healing may come with the action.

Another way of building faith is to ask someone what they would say is their level of pain on a scale of 1 to 10, with 1 being hardly noticeable and 10 being excruciating. After the initial prayer, they are asked if there has been any change and, if so, what the pain level is now. The next step is to give thanks to God for the improvement and then to ask for more until zero is reached. I did this with a pastor in Colombia recently who had asked me to pray for his severe back pain. He went from 9 to 2 to 1 and then, after doing a short exercise routine to test it out (see above), he pronounced himself pain free.

One more example of faith activation by those ministering would be having the boldness to test out what could be a 'word of knowledge' dropped into your mind by Holy Spirit. Just responding to any kind of Holy Spirit prompting requires an act of faith because you are rarely absolutely sure if it is Holy Spirit or not until you do something about it!

WHOLESALE HEALING

Smith Wigglesworth adopted this term when he ministered healing to a whole group at once rather than individually. In some cities or countries, he was forbidden to lay hands on people or to 'practise medicine without a licence', as they would have described his ministry. He circumvented such enemy-inspired restrictions by 'praying' for people *en masse*, without laying hands on any of them, and God healed them all together.

In a church meeting or a conference someone may minister through the 'word of knowledge' and several people could respond to the same word. Reasonable time constraints alone may mean it is impractical to minister to each one individually, unless there is a very large ministry team. If so, they can be 'prayed' for as a group. God does not find this tiring!

Sometimes a speaker in a meeting or a conference will give testimony to a specific healing he or she has previously witnessed and be prompted to ask if there is anyone now present who has the same problem or condition.

I have been in meetings where Bill Johnson has been the speaker and more than 50 people have raised their hands to say they have the same condition he has just described as having seen healed! He just called for them all to stand up to receive ministry together. (Randy Clark operates similarly.)

This could be achieved by asking people to come out either to him or to ministry team members to lay hands on them while he 'prays'. To direct attention away from himself, though, Bill usually asks people nearby to 'pray' for those who have stood up. After all, it is Holy Spirit who heals, albeit with the co-operation of the speaker!

One occasion I remember centred on a condition that the affected person still carried because of an injury sustained back in childhood. The meeting was in Tonbridge, England, and one of the many who received complete healing was a lady in her seventies, originally from Asia, who had fallen down some steps when she was a small child in her homeland! Well, we do serve the God of the (apparently) impossible!

BE NATURAL

We should beware religious posturing when we are ministering to the sick. Personally, I struggle with the sight of hands hovering in the air over someone being ministered to. It looks weird (to me, anyway), but don't worry about it if it doesn't to you!

I have heard, though it just might be apocryphal, that this phenomenon is due to people copying the practice of the John Wimber/Vineyard teams who first came to the UK in the 1980s. They ministered with raised, hovering hands but, it seems, they adopted this practice during hot Californian summers when it was too hot for all concerned to cope comfortably with the laying *on* of hands! But it became a habit. Now I see it happening regularly in cold English churches in the bleak midwinter! As I say, it may just be me so don't let yourself be influenced unduly by something of comparatively little importance.

Still, it can be good to ask ourselves sometimes why we do the things we do. For example, some find it too easy to adopt unnatural 'religious' language so that they end up sounding like some Old Testament prophet with a 1662 English vocabulary! How can someone who is not (yet) a Christian, or even a young Christian who has never encountered the King James Version of the Bible, relate to that? We have so many modern translations in everyday language so let's stick to the current vernacular when we minister!

Particularly when ministering to non-Christians it is also important not to lapse into 'Christianese', the kind of jargon that is familiar to those used to a church environment but is merely gibberish to the many who are not. Obviously, relevant scripture verses may come to mind during ministry, but these should be shared with great sensitivity with someone who is not familiar with the Bible.

RELAXED ATMOSPHERE

When we are ministering to someone, we need him or her to be as relaxed and comfortable as possible, especially if they are unchurched people in an alien (to them) environment. Although, to be fair, some of the most nervous people I have seen come forward for ministry, usually reluctantly, are long-standing Christians. Sadly, they have invariably been used to a church culture in which healing is not on the agenda, possibly genuinely believing it all stopped at the end of Acts 28.

VENTRILOQUISM

One of the traditional parts of a ventriloquist's act involves drinking a glass of water while the dummy is (apparently) speaking. I liken this to someone who prays himself, or herself, while they are being ministered to. I have heard my friend David, kindly and wisely, suggest to such people that it is not an example of good manners to speak while you are 'drinking' (i.e. to pray while simultaneously receiving ministry from the Lord) so would they kindly stop and just receive what the Lord is giving them?

It is very common for Christians to do this and they really should be encouraged to stop. Not only does it distract them but those ministering to them as well, especially if they pray out loud. It may seem good and pious, but it is invariably counterproductive. If they insist on continuing, it may even be best to gently suggest that you will just have to leave them to their own devices. After all, they have come to receive ministry, so it is perfectly reasonable for the emphasis to be on receiving.

A SAFE PLACE

It is easier to make yourself vulnerable in an environment where you feel safe. So, it is important that the people who come to us for ministry feel safe and secure with us and we do everything we can to make that possible. Our aim is to facilitate an encounter between them and God, who loves them more than they will ever know. That does not stop some people from being fearful, so we need to reassure them that they are in His 'everlasting arms'. Always address them by name; so, if the person is a stranger to you at first, begin by initiating friendly introductions.

Our ministry to people should be an expression of love, compassion, honour and respect. They need to be made to *feel* special because that is what they *are* in God's sight, regardless of their problem or its cause. If we receive any kind of prophetic insight as we minister, we should deliver any such 'words' very sensitively, recognising that we could be wrong. Every word shared should be positive, encouraging and edifying (please read 1 Corinthians 14:3).

DISTRACTIONS

If the time of ministry takes place during a busy conference, there could be many people involved in a confined space. This means there will be much to catch the unfocused eye or ear. Try hard not to be distracted by what else is going on in the room. Your distraction will almost certainly be sensed by the prayee and, not only is it rude, but also it is dishonouring to them.

LESS IS MORE

Always be prepared to give a person the amount of time necessary, especially when you first encounter them. However, without ever appearing to hurry them, recognise that 'less is more' in this ministry. Long 'prayers', even with the greatest of eloquence, are rarely necessary. In fact, the actual healing should usually be the briefest aspect of your time with them. Focus on facilitating an encounter between them and God, and not on your words.

Cathy and I were teaching in a small-group meeting in France recently when *Alvin* arrived a little late. He hobbled in on crutches, having been injured the evening before when taking a football practice session with some youngsters. His left ankle was badly sprained and he was clearly in considerable pain, so much so that he was unable to settle in one place for long in the room. Towards the end of the meeting we encouraged the whole group to minister healing to him, something he was very keen to receive!

They were largely inexperienced people, so we asked them to gather around Alvin and pray a long and complicated prayer lasting around nine seconds – I suggested they simply say, 'Be healed in Jesus' name' (but in French, of course). Cathy persuaded him to part with his crutches and he stood very tentatively in the centre with just the big toe of his left foot touching the floor. It was too painful for him to put more weight on his foot.

I counted '*Un, deux, trois*', and the other 10 or 12 people present prayed. Seconds later, Alvin began to move his ankle very gently. Then he gradually put more weight on his foot until it was flat on the floor. Next he began to walk – and declared himself pain free! Hallelujah! On the following Sunday, during the church meeting, he got up and enthusiastically shared his testimony, to the glory of God. Less *is* more!

T.H.I.N.K

Be careful about everything you say and how you say it, how you give expression to your thoughts and feelings. Words are powerful, and we want ours to be helpful, so we should T.H.I.N.K. before we speak.

Is what we want to say **T**rue, **H**elpful, **I**nspiring, **N**ecessary, **K**ind?

YOUNG OR VULNERABLE PEOPLE

Please avoid ministering to under-18s without first obtaining the permission of a parent, guardian or carer, and always give that person the option to remain present throughout (but be wary of them becoming a distraction or 'leaking' see Luke 8:51-53 unbelief). Anyone who comes to you for healing ministry is, to some extent, vulnerable at that time, but clearly, some people are vulnerable because of their current life circumstances and it is vital to be very sensitive about this.

KNOW YOUR LIMITATIONS

We are not providing a safe place for anyone if we allow ourselves to take ministry beyond the *current* scope of our experience and/ or training. Always operate within what you know to be your current level of grace gifting and do not consider yourself to be a failure if you know you should be seeking help from someone more experienced than you. Your primary concern must be the person receiving ministry, not your own ego. If that seems a bit harsh, please put yourself in the position of the person you are ministering to and consider what you would prefer to happen if your positions were reversed.

AUTHORITY

We minister out of the authority that Jesus has delegated to us so, ultimately, we look to Him for guidance and for direction by Holy Spirit. Nevertheless, we should be aware that the leader of the church or group that we are ministering to has authority, under God, for the people in that environment and be sensitive to any constraints that might bring upon what we do. I think I have made it clear that we prefer guidelines to rules but, nevertheless, not all churches and leaders will share that view. They will also know their people better than we do if we are visitors.

If we are ministering somewhere other than our home church, we should remember that we are serving there and readily submit to the authority of the leader/leadership. If this means that certain things are not acceptable (to them at that time) we should be sensitive to this. We will almost certainly not be there to help them with any follow-up ministry that may become necessary.

It is obviously best to get some idea of the preferred 'boundaries' within the church environment where we are ministering before we start. In this way, it may be possible to deal with the leader's concerns in advance and decide, with him or her, how best to handle any situations that they would normally have concerns about should they arise later.

In short, we choose to respect the host church leaders' point of view, even if we would not normally agree with it ourselves. We will not be able to gently encourage them, by our example, into greater freedom if we deliberately go against their wishes. If you are not a leader you cannot change the culture, but you can influence it.

BE THANKFUL

Finally, let us always remember to say 'Thank you' to God when we are ministering. There is a definite two-fold purpose in this. First, we give thanks for every sign of improvement in a person's condition as we minister to them. This is a faith builder for more and complete healing as we are encouraged to continue ministering.

Secondly, saying 'Thank you' after praying, whether there are obvious signs of healing or not, is a statement of faith and scripture reminds us that

> without faith it is impossible to please God, because anyone who comes to him must believe that he exists and that he rewards those who earnestly seek him.
>
> (Hebrews 11:6)

Not all healings are instant. Some are gradual, and some may take place a few hours, or even days, after the actual ministry time.

These are the ones you do not always hear about because it is amazing how lax people can be in feeding back the encouragement that comes from hearing that God moved when you ministered healing even though the end 'result' was not immediately apparent.

So please remember to 'give thanks in all circumstances; for this is God's will for you in Christ Jesus' (1 Thessalonians 5:18).

NOTES

[1] In normal circumstances we would recommend that both those ministering and the one being ministered to remain standing throughout the time of ministering (unless he or she falls in the Spirit, of course!). This is because sitting down can provide a temptation to move into counselling mode, which is always best avoided. It also encourages the 'less is more' aspect of ministry.

If the person's condition means that standing is too painful or difficult for them then a chair should be provided, but those ministering are advised to remain unseated. However, it is more honouring to the one being ministered to if they manoeuvre their bodies into a position where eye contact can be easily maintained throughout, at least with the team member ministering and speaking at any given time.

ADDENDUM

In the following chapter, I provide a set of Healing Ministry Guidelines that Cathy and I have put together, combined from both other sources and our own experience, primarily for ministry teams. They should also be of some value to individuals or couples starting their journey into the 'more' that God has for them.

Each one of us needs to be teachable, whether we are an experienced leader or the newest recruit. I do not suggest for one moment that these guidelines are perfect. They come with a flexibility to be changed as our experience, insight and divine revelation increases. Nevertheless, they will serve as a reasonable starting point for anyone taking their first steps into healing ministry as part of normal everyday Christian life.

Alongside reading and observing such guidelines, we recommend that you attend as many relevant training events and conferences as possible. We also suggest that you read books by authors who have learned from years of experience about both the blessings and the pitfalls of this wonderful ministry. We pray that God will richly bless you as you step out, take Him at His Word, and seek to glorify our Lord Jesus.

'God is pleased when we believe, not (just) when we get it right.'

(Joaquin Evans)

Chapter 16

MINISTRY GUIDELINES

Does God give you his Spirit and work miracles among you because
you observe the law or because you believe what you heard?

(Galatians 3:5, NIV 1984)

GOD IS SOVEREIGN, AND IT IS ESSENTIAL to follow the leading of Holy Spirit rather than any man-made rules and regulations, however sensible and well-meaning they may be. In addition, it is important to avoid any possibility of automatically slipping into formulae based on what has worked successfully in the past.

However, just as we have benefited from receiving guidance and boundaries from others with greater experience, we hope and pray that the following will be of value to you if you are comparatively new to healing ministry. It is largely drawn from a set of model guidelines[1] that Cathy and I have put together, influenced by others who have helped us over the years.

We very much like the team aspect of ministry. It is good to learn and grow together and to share experience with new recruits as they join from time to time. Ongoing training and support is to be recommended and, these days, it has become necessary to be increasingly aware of the potential legal implications pertaining to whatever we do. Every church, certainly in the UK, now has some form of safeguarding protocols or procedures that must be seen to be observed by all in order not to fall foul of the law.

It is sad but true that there are cases that go to court, if they are not settled beforehand, where it seems that something may have gone wrong either during or following ministry! Having a practical set of guidelines, which everyone can adhere to, is one way of minimising the possibility of something going awry.

We do recognise that there is obvious tension in setting this alongside the sovereignty of God.

EAGLES 4031 MINISTRY TEAM GUIDELINES TEMPLATE

In offering these recommendations, we are conscious of the need to respect the authority invested in the leadership of individual churches and for each person to submit to the sovereignty of God. Holy Spirit must be our ultimate source of authority, as well as of inspiration, guidance and direction.

> God is Healing, so Healing is in the presence of God. Therefore, it is good for the team to meet early in the room in which they will minister, also in the room where the meeting is to take place, if separate. This is to share testimonies, to worship and to invoke the presence of God the Holy Spirit to build faith, to encourage one another, and to cultivate a holy atmosphere for the people attending the meeting to encounter immediately they arrive.

- We believe that it is the will of God to heal the sick and that healing is an expression of His unconditional love and amazing grace ('on earth as it is in heaven').

- We understand that the Greek word *sozo*, usually translated into English as 'salvation', embraces **forgiveness**, **healing** and **deliverance**.

- We know, from our Bibles, that Jesus tells us to heal the sick, not to pray for them.

- We recognise our total dependency upon Holy Spirit always and that our purpose is to facilitate a connection between God and the person ministered to at a deep level.

- We have authority in the name of Jesus and we always minister conscious of our position in Him, expressing this in commands and declarations (as Jesus did).

- We ensure that our own personal hygiene is exemplary (e.g. using deodorant, mints for fresh breath, general cleanliness).

- We appreciate that it is important for us to provide a 'safe place' in which the person can receive all that God has for them at that time.

- Our aim is always to express and release the love of God to those ministered to, so we give them our undivided attention (i.e. we are not easily distracted).

- We minister in pairs, at least one of us being of the same sex as the person who is receiving ministry. We try to avoid ministering one to one with a member of the opposite sex but, if there is no alternative, we minister where others can see us easily.

- We remain in communication with our ministry partner always and we are ready to switch, at appropriate times, between the 'leading' and 'supporting' roles.

- We try to get into the habit of always keeping our eyes open as we minister so that we can see what is happening and how the person may be responding, as well as facilitating good communication with our ministry partner.

- We offer words, thoughts or insights sensitively, recognising that we could be wrong.

- We understand the difference between compassion (positive) and sympathy (negative) and we will always put the emphasis upon encouragement and edification. We are aware that compassion can bring someone out of a problem, but sympathy leaves them in it.

- We express grateful thanks and praise to God at every sign of improvement in the person's condition, inviting them to do the same, as this builds faith (in everyone) for more of God's healing grace to be released.

- We remember to pray quietly for guidance and insights if we encounter any resistance or suspect that there may be a blockage to their healing being released.

- We avoid moving into areas of ministry that are beyond our experience or training, but rather remain within our grace gifting (e.g. we do not use Sozo 'tools' unless we are Sozo trained).

- We never consider it to be a sign of failure if we recognise the need to ask for help from someone more experienced than ourselves.

- We will encourage the person to be as relaxed as possible, always addressing them by name, and helping them to become aware of the loving presence of God.

- We realise it is important always to listen to the person as well as to Holy Spirit; nevertheless we honour them by giving first place to the needs they have expressed.

- Although we have no wish to give the person the impression that we do not have sufficient time for them, when it comes to 'praying' we recognise that 'less is more'.

- We recognise that compassion is 'love without judgement' so we endeavour not to express shock at anyone's disclosures, but to convey love and acceptance, and we will always respect confidentiality (except when the law requires otherwise and we have no option but to notify the authorities, via our leaders; e.g. in cases of abuse).

- We know that the laying on of hands is biblical, but we always ask for permission, being sensitive about where we place our hands and only touching someone in a restrained and appropriate manner, especially a member of the opposite sex. We accept that a hand on the shoulder is sufficient.

- We are aware of the possibility of the person falling in the Spirit, being ready to catch them and lower them to the ground carefully, seeking always to protect their dignity and modesty, especially women.

- We always try to avoid slipping into counselling mode and any possibility of the person becoming more dependent upon us than upon God.

- If a person begins to pray themselves, while we are ministering to them, we graciously ask them to stop and remind them that they are here to receive, and it is not possible to 'drink and talk' at the same time.

- We never minister to any young persons under 18 years of age without first obtaining permission from a parent, guardian or carer, always giving them the option to be present during the whole ministry time.

- We realise that not all manifestations are demonic. They can be signs of Holy Spirit at work or they can be the result of deep emotional pain being released, so we recognise the need for us to develop the gift of discernment, seeking help if necessary.

- We make ourselves aware of the church leadership's policy for dealing with the demonic and respect this. If it is permissible to proceed with deliverance we do so only if either we are suitably experienced and confident ourselves or there is such a leader or colleague available to help us. We will endeavour to take the person into a less public area for such ministry, if appropriate.

- We recognise that those adults considered to be 'vulnerable' should be treated with special respect, care and consideration. We also realise that all who come forward for ministry are 'vulnerable' to some extent.

- We know that some healing is instant, some is gradual, some is delayed; but we are confident that God always does something when we minister as He empowers us to.

We recognise the importance of getting together as a team, at the end of the meeting, to encourage one another with testimonies and to be 'brushed off',[2] especially if there has been any demonic activity and/or deliverance taking place.

NOTES

[1] For the latest version of the Eagles 4031 Ministry Team Guidelines Template, go to either www.eagles4031.org.uk or info@eagles4031.org.uk.

[2] 'Brushing off' is the term we use for breaking off from one another, in Jesus' name, anything of the enemy that may have tried to attach itself to us as we have ministered to people who either were or may have been demonised.

Chapter 17

NEXT STEPS?

As the body without the spirit is dead, so faith without
deeds is dead.

(James 2:26)

MANY YEARS AGO, BACK IN THE mid-1980s to be precise, I remember a visit from a team from John Wimber's Vineyard church family to the UK. I was present at meetings they were involved in both at Holy Trinity, Brompton, and at my (then) home church in Maidstone. There was much that was exciting and new to experience, but the one thing that really sticks in my mind to this day is what one of the team leaders said during a meeting. It was something my evangelical, with a touch of the charismatic, mindset of the day really needed to hear: 'Why do you set such store by *learning* new things when you are not actually *doing* the things you have already learned?'

God really spoke to me through these words and I could
see that my approach to the Christian faith, at the time, was
very much based on mind or intellect rather than on growing
spiritually into maturity, with the primary focus upon deepening
my personal relationship with God. To be fair, that was pretty
much the kind of church environment I had grown up in during
the preceding 15 years. It was all I knew and that may be where
you are right now.

The emphasis seemed to be more on what we had learned
than on what we had experienced. This is typical of the Greek
mindset that the Western church has embraced over the centuries.
Even the Pentecostal-type revivals of the last 100 years or so seem
to have been affected by that mindset eventually.

This contrasts with what we might call the Hebrew mindset,
at least as it relates to learning. Here we find an equal emphasis
on the practical, the *doing* part of learning. This was the method
that Jesus used to teach His disciples. 'Watch me while I do it;
now do it alongside me; then you do it by yourself.' Yes,
we still need a degree of theory, or theology, but let's make it
practical theology. It's not either the mind or the spirit but both/
and.

There are scriptural reminders of this in verses like 1 Corinthians 4:20: 'For the kingdom of God is not a matter of talk but
of power.' John Wimber's appeal to the church to do the 'stuff'
expresses the same thought!

Taking this into account, and assuming you have read right
through to this point, can I suggest that you need to be asking
yourself what your next step, or steps, should be? In other words,
'Where do I go from here?'

If you have not discovered anything that is new to you in these
pages, then my guess is that you are already living a Christian
lifestyle that incorporates healing ministry as a normal expression

of it, at least to some extent. Well, as a minimum, then, you could practise it to an even greater extent!

For those readers for whom much has been new to them, it is important for you to put into practice what you have been reading here. Try to find a church, or group, of like-minded people, and encourage one another to step outside your comfort zones into a 24/7 Kingdom lifestyle that reflects the life that Jesus demonstrated so that we might imitate (re-present) Him and bring glory to the Father by releasing the power and presence of Holy Spirit.

By way of summary, let me just remind you of a few scriptures and salient points that are true to the theme and purpose of this book. Remember also what James wrote while in serious and amusing mode:

> Anyone who listens to the word but does not **do** what it says is like someone who looks at his face in a mirror and, after looking at himself, goes away and immediately forgets what he looks like.

> (James 1:23–24)

So, to conclude these pages, I have taken the scriptures used to open each chapter of this book and added a few comments by way of reminder.

INTRODUCTION

> And these signs **will** accompany those who believe … they will place their hands on sick people, and they **will** get well.

> (Mark 16:17, 18, NIV 1984)

This was one of the verses that encouraged Cathy and me to step out into the healing ministry in ways we had not done before,

inspired by the powerful healing I experienced in May 2008. Each
one of us has a different story, of course, especially at the beginning,
but we can have a common goal. Ours is to see the whole church
wake up to the fact that Jesus is alive and doing, through His
church, everything (and more) that He did as recorded in the
Gospels. Hopefully, this book (and others like it that I encourage
you to read) will help you on your journey.

We all begin a bit like Abraham, called but not really knowing
where we are going. But, in obeying God, there is nothing to fear
and so much to enjoy. If we can absorb the truth that it is the will
of God to heal today and we are willing to 'step out of the boat',
we will see it happen in our own experience.

CHAPTER 1: HEALING TESTIMONY

Those who hope in the LORD will renew their strength.
They will soar on wings like eagles; they will run and not
grow weary, they will walk and not be faint.

(Isaiah 40:31)

Many people who have stepped out into the healing ministry have
done so because of receiving a healing miracle from God that
has dramatically impacted their own lives. My testimony of what
happened to me when I touched the TV screen and waved goodbye
to 10–11 years of ME (chronic fatigue) is an integral part of my
story. I hope that you have a personal story that is equally special
to you.

If healing is not your personal need, then I pray you will be
part of someone else's story of miraculous, life-changing healing
that will create in you a thirst for more of God and His grace.

Remember, as part of the worldwide Christian family it is perfectly legitimate to use the stories of brothers and sisters in Christ as testimonies of what God has done (and will do again) until you have your own experiences to relate. The latter are much more powerful when you share them because no one can negate the truth of a genuine 'God' experience, no matter how hard they might try. However, please do not use a person's *real* name unless you have first obtained their permission to do so.

CHAPTER 2: GOING OUT ON A LIMB

> Taking him by the right hand, [Peter] helped him up, and instantly the man's feet and ankles became strong.
>
> (Acts 3:7)

As we gain more experience of healing ministry it is possible that we will discover that we seem to have more 'success' with a certain kind of sickness or disability than with others. While that is no reason to stop pursuing God for healings in those other areas, it is worth noting (avoiding false humility) that God has given you a special anointing for this aspect.

Or, if you prefer to express it another way: you have greater expectancy that God will invariably heal a certain ailment because you are already well acquainted with His faithfulness in this area through regular experiences of His healing grace being released in the past.

In my case, it has proved to be misalignment of the skeletal system, and it is very rare indeed that nothing seems to happen when I minister to people with this sort of problem. It is also true of people who have one arm or leg shorter than the other, either because they were born that way or as a result of an operation to mend a fracture, for example.

What might it be for you? If you have no idea as you read this, just think how exciting and rewarding it will be finding out. There is nothing more satisfying and encouraging than to see God at work, especially when you have reached a level of faith that has moved well into confident expectation because of what you have already seen to date.

CHAPTER 3: WORDS OF KNOWLEDGE

> To one there is given through the Spirit ... the message [or word] of knowledge.
>
> (1 Corinthians 12:8b, NIV 1984)

We know that this is only one of nine spiritual gifts listed early in 1 Corinthians chapter 12 but it is a very important one in the healing ministry. We are encouraged, in chapter 14 of Paul's letter, to eagerly desire the spiritual.[1] Indeed, the original Greek word translated 'desire' apparently can be more accurately rendered as 'lust after', so strong is the encouragement given by the apostle!

There are other gifts which can be equally effective when ministering healing but this one particularly stands out. Not only can it be the means of God indicating to someone that He wants to deal with their problem, it can also be a means of breakthrough when some sort of obstruction to healing is encountered during a time of ministry. Either way it serves as a faith builder.

If this is new to you, then I recommend that you 'practise' with a small group of like-minded people. Get into a group where there will be plenty of mutual encouragement – and only constructive criticism if you get it 'wrong' during the learning process. The secret is always to be willing to share even the most seemingly ridiculous 'words' without fear of looking a fool. Fear of other people is at the root of that, whereas God is pleased with us for trying even when we (seem to) get it 'wrong'. As the song says, He is such a 'good, good Father'.

CHAPTER 4: THE THREE 'I'S: IDENTITY + INTIMACY = IMPACT

> Therefore, if anyone is in Christ, the **new creation** has come: the old has gone, the new is here!
>
> (2 Corinthians 5:17)[2]

I have explained how we have learned the importance of the Three 'I's (Identity + Intimacy = Impact) and this verse deals with the first of those three. It is vital to know our identity in Christ, who we really are in Him. It is then that we have a better idea of what it is to be self-confidently confident in Him and all He is ready, willing and able to do both in and through us.

We can be so keen to demonstrate that we do not have a higher opinion of ourselves than we should that the humility we display can be false rather than genuine. Being overly conscious of our past failures and weaknesses means we can lose sight of what Paul, inspired by Holy Spirit, is telling us here.

The 'old' has gone! We are born again of the Spirit, newly created in Him. The fruit of our lives and the fruit of the Spirit can be one and the same. The gifts we use to accomplish what the Lord has called us to do and the gifts of the Spirit can be one and the same, too. Frankly, it is humbling to know who we are because every good thing we have is received by grace; grace being 'undeserved favour'.

> You, God, are my God, earnestly I seek you; I thirst for you, my whole being longs for you, in a dry and parched land where there is no water. I have seen you in the sanctuary and beheld your power and your glory. Because your love is better than life, my lips will glorify you. I will praise you as long as I live, and in your name I will lift up my hands.

> (Psalm 63:1–3)

The Lord longs for us to draw nearer to Him. To know intimacy of relationship with Him is His own idea. For some this seems to be a little threatening, especially at first. But, as we come to terms with who we are in Christ, so we become more aware of our deep need to be ever closer to Father (or Daddy) God.

He loves us so much, more than mere words can express, and it is our privilege to be able to reflect that love back to Him. Quiet times alone with Him; worshipping Him in spirit and in truth, whether alone or in the company of our church family; all are vitally important to our growth into greater maturity as Christians.

Jesus only said what He 'heard' the Father saying and only did what He 'saw' the Father doing. His life was the outworking of His amazing intimacy with His Father. He has modelled what is possible for us, and our perseverance in this area will be richly rewarded.

> Now Stephen, a man full of God's grace and power, performed great wonders and signs among the people.

> (Acts 6:8)

Stephen, whose only recorded role in the church was as a distributor of daily food to the Hellenic widows, performed great signs and wonders. His life obviously involved a little more than what happened around mealtimes! He could do mighty works because this was the impact, the outworking of the grace and power of God in him, which can only have resulted from knowing who he was in Christ and having an intimate relationship with God: Father, Son and Holy Spirit. Stephen is an example of what is possible both for you and for me.

CHAPTER 5: HEAVEN'S HEALTH MANIFESTO

Praise the LORD, O my soul, and forget not all his benefits – who forgives all your sins and heals all your diseases.

(Psalm 103:2–3)

The wonderful thing about the healing grace of God is that it has always been available, even under the Old Covenant. His perfect will and purpose for the lives of His children was spelled out right from the beginning of the scriptures. The Israelites missed out on so much simply through their disobedience and unbelief. It is so important that we do not allow ourselves to fall into the same traps, either deliberately or through ignorance. Doubt and unbelief are not the same – unbelief is a choice.

Sadly, there is still a large element of the church that either refuses, or struggles, to accept all that God has provided for us in His amazing grace. My subject, in this book, is healing but there is so much more that this applies to. If we will just allow ourselves to be influenced more by the Word of God than any negative experiences to date, we will be able to break through into all the wonders of our glorious inheritance here on earth. His provision is vast, and His resources are infinite.

CHAPTER 6: AUTHORITY

All authority in heaven and on earth has been given to me.
Therefore [you] go and …

(Matthew 28:18–19)

The victory of Jesus won back from the devil all that the latter
had taken from mankind by his original deception of Adam and
Eve. Jesus has all authority, which, by my calculations, means that
the devil now has none! The devil only holds sway over us to the
degree that we come into agreement with him, more specifically
with his lies.

Jesus demonstrated time and again that He had authority over
sickness and all the wiles of the enemy. It is His authority that we
employ as we step out in faith, and in His footsteps, to 'destroy the
devil's work' (1 John 3:8). He did not call us to pray for the sick
but to heal the sick and that is possible only by using the authority
He has delegated to us.

Those whom He calls He also equips and there is a whole load
of 'good works' He has lined up for us to do in bringing healing to
the sick and freedom to the oppressed (Ephesians 2:10).

CHAPTER 7: THE FULL GOSPEL

Therefore, go and make disciples of all nations, baptising
them in the name of the Father and of the Son and of the
Holy Spirit, and teaching them to obey everything I have
commanded you.

(Matthew 28:19–20)

This is a particularly useful scripture for confounding those who
believe what I, and others, consider to be the false doctrines of

cessationism and dispensationalism. Adherents contend that signs and wonders, including healing, have already fully served their purpose and are not for today.

Here we have a command from Jesus, first to the original apostles, to teach every new disciple (to the end of the age) to obey the commands that He gave to them. Look once again at Matthew 10:7–8, for example. They were required to pass on the baton to each subsequent generation of believers until Jesus returns. Which means that you and I are intended to pick it up.

CHAPTER 8: HOPE, FAITH AND EXPECTANCY

You may ask me for **anything** in my name, and I will do it.

(John 14:14)

There are at least two different ways of looking at this verse. On the one hand, it could be a particularly difficult verse to take on board and act upon. On the other hand, being a promise of Jesus, it could be as true, and as valid, as any of His many other promises.

I have used it to distinguish between faith and expectation, when expectation is that 'knowing it will happen' kind of faith that the early disciples, and many others down the centuries, have exhibited. This could be either the 'gift of faith', mentioned in the list of nine spiritual gifts in 1 Corinthians 12, or a high level of expectation based upon the regularly observed faithfulness of God.

There seem to be no preconditions expressed about this promise. Indeed, it follows on from the verse, much quoted in this book, about believers doing the same works that Jesus did – and even greater works. If there are any preconditions, are they not only that one should be a believer, both in Him and of His

great and precious promises (2 Peter 1:4), and in right relationship with Him?

Nevertheless, experience shows that few believers move straight
into such a totally confident prayer/ministry life. In my view, such
a high level of confidence would correlate with the level of intimacy
found in a disciple's relationship with God. Is it close enough to
'see' clearly what the Father is doing and to 'hear' clearly what
the Father is saying?

I believe that the key is our relationship with Him being one
which is close enough to discern the will of God in a matter before
making our requests known to Him. In this context, I think it is
fair to say that we all remain a work in progress. We will move
on if we are both determined and persistent, ready and willing to
'press in' for the 'more' of God by taking R.I.S.K.

CHAPTER 9: DEALING WITH DISAPPOINTMENT

Therefore, since through God's mercy we have this ministry,
we do not lose heart.

(2 Corinthians 4:1)

Yes, we will make progress and see many wonderful things happen
as the Kingdom of God is manifested around us, but that does not
mean that we will never encounter disappointment. Only Jesus has
a 100% 'success' rate in ministering healing, so some disappointment is inevitable for each one of us, unless or until we reach His
level. The important thing is that we do not allow this to dishearten
us, to cause us to lose hope. We need to remain positive and persistent in following the call of God upon our lives.

If you read biographies of the many who have been used
greatly by God to heal the sick, you will be both surprised and
encouraged to find how many of them went on ministering to

the sick for years before seeing a breakthrough. A combination of conviction and persistence won through, and the development of character through overcoming disappointment meant that God could trust them with more and greater works.

CHAPTER 10: DEALING WITH OPPOSITION

> For our struggle is not against flesh and blood ... but against the authorities, against the powers of this dark world and against the spiritual forces of evil in the heavenly realms.
>
> (Ephesians 6:12)

Every Christian ministry encounters opposition, all too often from within the church. It is so very easy to fall out with people who disagree with us; who can be difficult at times; who may even go so far as to persecute us. But, when push comes to shove, they are not the real opposition, the real enemy.

Every move of God, every single church, every individual Christian has one implacable enemy: the devil (and his minions). Ultimately, our struggle is with them. They are the actual root of the opposition we will encounter, and we will do well to remember that. It is not too difficult for our enemy to find people to work through to achieve his ends, often without the people being aware that they are co-operating with him in this 'war'. The good news, of course, is that we are being opposed by an already defeated enemy who is disarmed, having lost the authority he stole from mankind at the Fall.

This enemy can only hold sway over us to the degree that we come into agreement with him and his lies. By experience, we will come to learn more about the wiles of the enemy. Our ability to discern will increase. Knowing who we are in Christ and drawing

ever closer to God, His rich provision and His promises, makes us
more confident in this conflict. 'Submit yourselves, then, to God.
Resist the devil, and he will flee from you' (James 4:7–8).

CHAPTER 11: OPEN HEAVENS

> You shall see heaven open, and the angels of God ascending
> and descending on the Son of Man.
>
> (John 1:51)

Through Jesus, we have been provided with access direct to the
throne room of Heaven. When our relationship with God is as
strong and as healthy as He has already provided for it to be,
nothing can come between Heaven and us. There are times when
the presence, the anointing, of God is so strong, so tangible, that it
must be very much like being in Heaven itself. This is what Jacob
encountered in Genesis 28; what Jesus described to Nathanael in
the verse above. Such an experience can be yours and mine, too.

Usually, we will come into an experience like this in a time of
personal or corporate worship, but it can and often does carry over
into public ministry. Therefore, I have readily passed on to you
what blessings have resulted in ministries like the Healing Centre
when time has been spent in worship and encountering the tangible
presence of God before moving on to minister to the sick. We are
privileged carriers of the Presence!

CHAPTER 12: ACTS 29

> In my former book, Theophilus, I wrote about all that Jesus
> **began** to do and teach …
>
> (Acts 1:1 and 'Acts 29')

The four Gospels contain exciting accounts of all the things that Jesus, the Son of Man, began to do and teach. The book of Acts deals, in the early part of chapter 1, with the resurrection of Jesus. From verse 10 of chapter 1 through to the end of chapter 28, the first disciples no longer have His physical presence with them. So, if the Gospels only deal with what Jesus *began* to do, then what He *continued* to do He did through believers who were empowered by Holy Spirit. As if to confirm this, we have the account of the first Holy Spirit baptism in Acts chapter 2.

You will have gathered by now that I totally disagree with anyone who continues to teach and/or believe that what Jesus began in the Gospels, and what Holy Spirit continued to do throughout the book of Acts, was only intended by God to take place during the first century AD or, as some would have it, until the canon of the New Testament was finalised about 250 years later. Jesus told His disciples that they would do what He had done, and even greater things, but He also told them to continue to make new disciples and to teach them to do those same things. All His teachings are to be passed on through all generations.

'Acts 29' began at the end of Acts 28 and will continue until Jesus returns. All that is accomplished in the name of Jesus, by the power of Holy Spirit, to the glory of God the Father, will be recorded in Heaven. I like to think it is possible that those records are kept under the banner heading of something like 'Acts 29'! The title is not the point, of course: what is actually recorded is the crux of it all. You and I, and every other Christian believer, are called to do the works of Jesus in this world, to demonstrate to people that the Kingdom of Heaven is, and continues to be, at hand. And not just to people either!

His intent was that now, through the church, the manifold wisdom of God should be made known to the rulers and authorities in the heavenly realms, according to his eternal purpose that he accomplished in Christ Jesus our Lord. In him and through faith in him we may approach God with freedom and confidence.

(Ephesians 3:10–12)

CHAPTER 13: HIS PRESENCE

And surely I am with you always, to the very end of the age. (Matthew 28:20)

If we are to be effective representatives of Jesus here on earth, we must know that we are carriers of His presence. Peter, inspired by Holy Spirit, goes so far as to say:

His divine power has given us everything we need for a godly life through our knowledge of him who called us by his own glory and goodness. Through these he has given us his very great and precious promises, so that through them you may **participate in the divine nature**, having escaped the corruption in the world caused by evil desires.

(2 Peter 1:3–4)

That is surely the definition of one who carries the presence of God. We know that it is true because it is in the Bible, but the application of it can be another matter. In this case, being aware of the possibility of such a privilege is equally vital. Then, of course, we need to believe it is true for both you and me to step out in faith accordingly; so that our faith is seen in action.

A politician once responded to a noisy heckler, during an election campaign, with the words: 'Madam, I can only give you the facts.

I cannot give you the intellectual capacity with which to appreciate them!' God gives us His promises, He calls us to action, He empowers us to do what He has called us to, but our co-operation is essential for the mission to be accomplished. We cannot possibly do it without Him and He does not want to do it without us!

CHAPTER 14: STEPPING OUT (A CASE STUDY)

> One day Peter and John were going up to the temple at the time of prayer ...

> (Acts 3:1–26)

In this chapter I sought to use the account of Peter and John and the beggar at the Beautiful Gate of the temple in Jerusalem to illustrate, from the Bible, how these apostles (believers) modelled what I have tried to convey through these pages. Some may accuse me of using a little 'poetic licence' here and there but I believe that I have written nothing which conflicts with the tone of scripture and the purposes of God for His children today as we pursue what has been passed down to us over the generations since the time of the events described. You must be the judge of that.

CHAPTER 15: HOW TO HEAL THE SICK?

> Heal the sick who are there and tell them, 'The kingdom of God is near you.'

> (Luke 10:9, NIV 1984)

I have explained that I am not very comfortable with the 'How to ...' variety of Christian books and I had no wish to make this book into a manual about how to heal the sick. I am not qualified to do that; if for no other reason than I am not an expert and only great experts should write 'How to ...' books. The Bible is a great manual and, as we know, it was inspired by the ultimate Expert!

Instead I have simply tried to recount a few experiences, in the hope that they will be helpful, also providing words of advice, along with suggestions and recommendations. If my experience to date is a little more extensive than yours, I trust you will have found something helpful and encouraging within these pages. Indeed, I pray you will build your floor on my ceiling.

I have emphasised that there are no rules, as such. If you genuinely seek to share the Lord's love and compassion for people, and to minister accordingly, you cannot go far wrong. More importantly, you will be in the will of God and there is no better and safer place to be, both for you and the people you minister to.

> We all have to learn to start our own fire [i.e. to put into practice what we have learned].
>
> (Steve Backlund)

Thank you for allowing me to share my thoughts and experiences with you. May God richly bless you as you step out of your comfort zone, place yourself in His gentle but powerful hands, and soar like an eagle in the Kingdom of Heaven, as His healing ministry becomes an increasingly significant part of your normal, everyday Christian life.

A good friend of ours, wonderfully used in healing ministry, both inside and outside the church walls, has given a short and very powerful summary of what is required: Love – Presence – Risk. We take the Love of God with us, we operate out of rest in His Presence, and we are willing to take a Risk (an alternative spelling of Faith).

Finally, do you think your church family might benefit from a weekend of 'Acts 29' with Eagles 4031? If so, Cathy and I would love to hear from you, or from your church or group leader. Check out either our website or our ministry Facebook page for more information and contact details.

NOTES

[1] It is interesting to note that, in the original Greek, there is no word for what has been translated as 'gifts' in either 1 Corinthians 12:1 or 1 Corinthians 14:1. The word 'spiritual' alone is a more accurate rendering. Of course much of the context is focused on 'gifts' but, in my view, Paul is actually directing us towards living a 24/7 spiritual lifestyle which will incorporate the 'gifts'.

[2] Scriptures for the Three 'I's in this section are not those used to introduce the subject in Chapter 4.

Lightning Source UK Ltd.
Milton Keynes UK
UKHW020040121021
392037UK00008B/1606